THE ADVENTURES OF
A CURIOUS
CAT

CURIOUS ZELDA

AND MATT TAGHIOFF

SPHERE

First published in Great Britain in 2019 by Sphere
This paperback edition published in 2020 by Sphere

3 5 7 9 10 8 6 4 2

A CIP catalogue record for this book is available from the British Library.

ISBN 978-0-7515-8119-5

Printed and bound in Great Britain by Bell and Bain Ltd, Glasgow

Papers used by Sphere are from well-managed forests
and other responsible sources.

Sphere
An imprint of
Little, Brown Book Group
Carmelite House
50 Victoria Embankment
London EC4Y 0DZ

An Hachette UK Company
www.hachette.co.uk

www.littlebrown.co.uk

For Oliver
The tiniest explorer I know

THE RESCUE

My name wasn't always Zelda. And I wasn't always this way. When I was a kitten, my mother told me all the old stories and warned me about being too curious. Adventures took time away from the important strings in life, and were best left to other cats.

Then, one day, my life changed. I don't remember much other than a few fleeting smells – the plastic of the carrier. The warm, nutty aroma of the back seat of the car. Sitting on a desk beside some flowers. A kindly human who faintly smelled of mackerel carrying me to my new room.

At first, I assumed it was a sort of hotel. Although the facilities were a little basic, the kindly human did indeed bring me mackerel from time to time. Beyond that, my nose picked up precious little. Other humans often came in looking confused as nobody knew which cat was theirs, despite a lot of frantic mewing. Still, everyone usually worked it out between themselves and each cat would happily leave with their humans. But my humans never came.

Weeks passed and I began to suspect something wasn't right. Why wasn't *I* leaving? I tried to hatch a plan with Fluffles in the neighbouring cage, with limited success. He was a compulsive napper. I realised that my only hope of escape was to convince a human that they were mine.

I missed several opportunities as visitors often caught me at the wrong time, either when I was hiding or licking something interesting off the floor. Eventually a suitable family walked in. I scurried to the front of my cage, trying to get their attention. They . . . laughed. I was crestfallen. They moved on and picked a handsome tabby who was, if I'm honest, a bit self-absorbed. Typical. I continued working on my presentation, doing my stretches, keeping my claws sharp and my nose wet. It was vital to stay on high alert and sniff out opportunities before my peers if I was to get noticed. I kept trying.

Then, one day, I overheard a member of hotel staff in the distance. 'Don't be put off by her spooked expression.' A pair of humans emerged and headed straight towards me. I noticed one of them was furrier than the other. I mewed sweetly and widened my eyes, locking my gaze with theirs.

'Wow...she has the *silliest* expression I've ever seen!' said the furry one.

'I think she's quite fond of you,' said the other. I guess it was true, and I continued rubbing my face on him.

'We'll take her.'

Don't I get a say? I pondered, as the fish lady picked me up. It didn't matter – I had done it! There were of course some formalities. Before committing to anything, I insisted on visiting their residence to ensure its suitability. The journey was very stop-start, frighteningly loud and shaky, but that's the London Underground for you.

My first steps in my new territory were a little overwhelming. When the door to my carriage opened, I tiptoed out and stood for a few moments, taking it all in before starting an intensive survey. The place seemed in good order, with plenty of soft furnishings. I began inspecting the carpet, moving onto upholstered furniture, and finally ensuring that all corners, nooks, and hideaways were present and correct.

I retreated to a more secluded area underneath the sofa, where I could peacefully consider my findings. The furry human knelt down and looked at me. 'How about . . . *Zelda?*' he asked. I was terrified, and yet I couldn't stop staring back. As he rolled a small treat over to me, I knew my ordeal was over. I was home.

Living Curiously

All of this was many moons ago; my life now is very different. The time since my rescue has been a huge learning curve with many ups and downs, but I'm pleased to say my humans are gradually getting up to speed.

I've had to adapt too, for it was only once I'd left the shelter that I realised I'd led a sheltered life. Over time, I've learnt how to harness my natural inquisitiveness. It's one thing to spend an evening sprinting around a living room in a blur of upholstery, but how many of us ever stop and really smell the couch cushions?

There's just so much to explore in the great indoors. I'll always love whiling away a few blissful hours in the sock drawer, but this life has opened my eyes, even wider than before. I'm making new findings every day, and I can't wait any longer to start sharing them with the world.

Learning to hold a pen hasn't been straightforward. After many hours of practice, my mouth began to ache. Overcoming writer's jaw was just one of many challenges I've faced. But as with all great literature, if my writing inspires even one other cat to dip a first cautious paw in the water, it will have all been worth it.

First I heard it
Then I looked
Think I saw it
Now I'm hooked

ADVICE FOR CATS

LIVING WITH HUMANS

I want to start with a very important topic: Humans. If you think you can maintain an active lifestyle on your own, it's time to wake up and smell the coffee table. Behind every successful cat, there are at least one or two members of dedicated staff. These humans take an unbelievable amount of looking after for such simple creatures, but much like a laundry basket, you only get out what you put in.

Most of the time, what they're really after is your approval. Knowing they have it does wonders for their self-esteem, and it's tempting to go overboard. Get the balance right, though, and you'll have their loyalty and gratitude for ever. They'll brush your coat, empty your litter tray and bring you all the food you can inhale.

Curiosity is contagious, and I've noticed my sense of adventure has rubbed off on my humans. When I first arrived, they barely had a reason to get out of bed. Now, they're *so* much happier – you can really see the wonder in their eyes as I swat them awake in the morning. In fact, the more time I spend with them as they're getting ready, the more invigorated they get, eagerly zipping around the house and flying out of the door to seize the morning.

Our relationship wasn't always so functional. Since we've been cohabiting, I've deduced that humans have a number of strange habits. It is therefore crucial that you know how to handle these in order to set the right tone and avoid disaster.

Communication

Humans enjoy watching and talking to their cats, even if it isn't reciprocal. They'll begin their advances by calling your name, growing louder and more desperate with each repetition. Always ensure that you look away during these moments until the graceless calling subsides. I find that a blank wall is the ideal distraction.

Contact

Some humans may encroach on your personal space and attempt to touch you. These awkward encounters can be tricky to judge, and most humans will need a bit of direction on their petting technique. Once they've performed a few strokes, let them know how they're doing by either purring or scratching them.

Territory

You may have noticed that your home is divided into a number of distinct areas. While almost any surface is an appropriate resting place for a cat, humans aren't like that. They will sleep only in a bed or on your couch, eat only at a table or facing a TV, and bizarrely will clean themselves only in a dedicated container. Don't let their restrictions deter you: whether you fancy napping on the side table, eating the bug by the window or washing yourself in the doorway, your territory has no limits.

Boundaries

In order to properly run a household, you need to set clear boundaries. The couch is yours. All chairs, stools, ottomans, cushions, beds, benches and rugs are also yours. One great way of asserting your ownership is by marking these items. Getting fur all over them is a classic way to claim your space, while a bit of clawing adds a personal touch. If you catch humans using your furniture, try staring at them disapprovingly.

Safe Spaces

Homes are filled with unpredictable goings on. Strange noises, distinct smells, and visitors should all be approached with caution. Sometimes it will become necessary to retreat in order to avert danger. Ensure that you have a paw-ful of readily accessible hiding places in any given area. High places offer an ideal vantage point, and a great way to look down on your humans!

FOOD

Life with humans opens up many opportunities for sustenance. For all their shortcomings, humans are blessed with the ability to operate a tin opener. This technique guarantees you a satisfyingly mushy meal on demand, especially on those days off from hunting. If you're dieting, some humans can provide salad, also known as plants. Patrol the windowsills regularly, as they'll need your help pruning them; a quick nibble on the fern is not just a fresh snack, but a key step to a blossoming relationship with your humans.

TRAINING

All humans need guidance in order to fulfil their duties. I made the following instructions for mine, and I urge you to do the same for yours . . .

ZËLDA

1 Always leave your Zelda in the folded position

2 Please be careful not to overcharge your Zelda

3 Always check the voltage before using your Zelda

 Always wear clothes when greeting your Zelda

 Approach carefully, preferably with food

 Never forget to remind her that it's not the apocalypse

They say curiosity killed the cat . . . Do you find this startling? Because I do! I often find myself overwhelmed by life, electrified by the idea that panic could strike at any moment. There's just so much excitement to be found in the everyday jitters: not knowing what's for breakfast, the unexpected ring of a doorbell, the stress of brush hour. I've found that being startled is the ticket to all sorts of thrills and spills – and I've got the butterflies in my stomach to prove it.

Not everyone can be as highly strung as I am, but if this sounds frightfully familiar, then concatulations: you're in the Startled Cats Club. Now WATCH OUT! There's a few rules to overbear in mind:

- I will remain on high alert at all times
- I promise not to blink during waking moments
- I vow not to fully close my eyes during sleep
- I will exercise caution when walking on tiled flooring
- I will hide under the sofa in response to new sounds
- I promise not to greet visitors who show an interest in me
- I vow not to enter a room with a live extractor fan
- I will focus intently on all moving things
- I will focus intently on all stationary things
- I accept no responsibility for items damaged during frantic scrambles
- I promise to panic during changes of wind direction
- I vow never to be within 10 feet of a vacuum cleaner
- I consent to having daily existential crises

ZELDA THE COOK

Cats are very independent. We like being able to look after ourselves and do things on our own terms. Although I may not have shown it in the past, I've always been career driven. The change in my routine will be drastic, but now I'm truly ready to begin part-time work. I've even been practising my interview technique in front of the microwave, and I can just feel the confidence radiating from me.

I need a job
I'll take a look
I found a hob
I'm now a cook

Full English Wreckfast

English people are famous for the food they eat at the start of the day. However, I have found their tastes very peculiar, especially their reliance on stripey pig strips and chicken splats. For this recipe, there's no need to do any cooking. All you need is a bit of skill to recreate my twist on a popular classic:

First, wait for your human to sit down at the table. Next, jump on the table and stare at their food for as long as you can hold out. Your human may say things like 'That's not for you' and 'Why are you still staring?'. Ignore them. It is for you to take. Extend your paw and gently nudge their food along the plate. Spear a morsel with your claw and seize it. When your human reacts, make a dash off the table, knocking over the orange juice as you flee.

Spaghetti with foil balls

This is a traditional dish in many cat households requiring plenty of string; much more than the strand your human occasionally waves in front of your face. You will have ideally amassed a good hoard over the years, but if you're running low, you can simply steal some from your human. Head to your local shoe rack for the latest selection.

To accompany your string, foil balls are particularly curious objects, as they are impossible to produce without thumbs. If you need them made to order, let your human know by biffing them in the face. If you cannot locate your human, you may be able to find a healthy supply underneath your sofa.

As with most of my recipes, there's very little cooking involved. After all, good spaghetti should be like the furniture in my home: All Denty. Start by heating your water bowl up to room temperature. Then plonk your string in the bowl and wait for your human to fish it out. Top with foil balls and tuck in. Buon Appawtito!

Loaf of Bread

There's nothing like a freshly baked loaf on a Caturday morning. This recipe is as divine as it is simple. There's no flour, salt, yeast or water involved – you only need yourself. Make sure your work surfaces are clear before you start baking, by knocking everything off the kitchen countertops. Do the same with the coffee table, just in case.

Next, move to a fabric surface and arch your back, stretching like dough until your ears begin to flutter. Plant your claws into the fabric and begin kneading, working the area around you to create the right baking conditions. Next, slowly lower yourself into a crouched position and carefully tuck each limb underneath your belly. Bake at room temperature for approximately ages. You are now a loaf of bread.

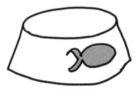

Catsu Curry

Curry was originally discovered by a curious cat who knocked over the spice rack. While staff cleared away the wreckage, a unique blend of flavours combined and inspired a dish prepared in many kitty kitchens today.

The beauty of this recipe is in its simplicity – any curry can become a catsu curry, and it's a real clowder pleaser. Wait for your human to finish preparing their curry, and then step in it. Magically, you will have created catsu curry. Your human will be delighted to see that you've improved their favourite dinner, cheering you on with a rallying cry.

Sashimi

Sashimi, also known as 'Fish', is always best served fresh. For this dish, you will require either a pond or a fish tank. If you have one nearby, this recipe will be a piece of hake. Start by lowering your paw into the water, and carefully scoop the sashimi up using your claws. Your catch may be a little startled at first, but it will soon calm down.

Some chefs can be a bit finicky with preparation, slicing and rolling it up with mice to make sushi. I much prefer to eat mine whole and fast. If you do want to add flavour, there is nothing wrong with dipping it in koi sauce first.

Bagel

The bagel is one of the most challenging bread products to make. After years of experimentation, I have managed to formulate a recipe guaranteed to yield a bagel every time. Follow my instructions carefully and get ready for some holesome baking:

1) Find a large bowl

2) Step inside and curl up asleep

3) Rest for 180 minutes

4) You are now a bagel

It is important that you are not distracted during the lengthy baking process. I would therefore recommend clearing the house of any humans, insects or plants before you begin.

CLOSE TO MY HEART

Curly arms. Thready face.
Squidgy lap. Sturdy base.
Chunky feet. Warm embrace.
Always there. Just in case.

— 'Armchair'

Tall and shiny. Bottom frosty.
Wide and heavy. Face reflecty.
So silence. Den loud.
Tiny feet. Best friend.

— 'Fridge'

Long legs. No feet.
Brown face. Can't eat.
Hard chest. Soft head.
My friend. My bed.

— 'Piano stool'

24

TOP 5 EXERCISES FOR CATS

CIRCUIT TRAINING

Best practised during the daily mad half hour, circuit training can be exhausting. Make sure that you drink plenty of water in advance; I find that any vessel other than your water bowl will suffice. Starting in the room you last napped in, sprint across the hallway into the next, vaulting over any items of furniture in your path. When you reach the second room, come to a sudden stop. Hold for one second and glance at your human. Then race back to the room you started in. Repeat process until the half-hour is up, or you become distracted.

25

YOGA

Yoga was discovered thousands of years ago by a man standing on one leg, praying not to fall over. As he crashed to the ground, his cat got startled and arched her back. It was at this moment that the 'cat stretch' was born. Shortly after, the cat also sunk her claws into the man's exercise robe, although sadly this move is seldom practised in yoga today.

Whether you want to improve your balance on the bookshelf, or increase agility when cleaning yourself, yoga is essential to kitty fitness. Begin with a stretch, securing all four sets of claws on any fabric surface. Next, sit back and hoist one leg in the air, licking your butt for 10 seconds. Move onto your side and into the shrimp position, grabbing both of your feet, and lick them for 10 seconds. Finally, curl into a ball and go to sleep – *Namastay* for as long as you wish.

CURTAIN CLIMBING

Have you ever noticed how infrequently your humans climb the curtains at home? Most of them shy away from the sport. It's not that they're unable to, but people are great at finding excuses not to exercise. You'll often hear them say 'I'm too busy to climb the curtains' or 'I'll start next week'. Some never even make it to the windowsill, which is precisely why they are unfit.

There is nothing quite like the feeling of scaling a curtain, planting each claw in the fabric and pulling yourself up to glory. You may hear gasps from spectators observing your ascent, but the views are amazing at the top. You might be wondering if this activity could damage the curtains. Fear not, for your humans are committed to keeping your exercise equipment in top condition. They'll be the first to discover any loose threads or tears, and will reward you with a nice new pair every so often.

LEAP OF FAITH

Are *you* bored of being on the floor? Need an adrenaline rush? If you answered *yes* to both questions, you may be ready to take a leap of faith. This sport involves death-defying jumps to those hard-to-reach places you've always dreamt of visiting in your home. Perhaps there's a shelf that you can't easily get to, or a wardrobe that seems a bit too tall for its own good. Or maybe you've already arrived at your high vantage point, and you're reading this while balancing on top of a door.

The best thing about this sport is that you don't need any training or safety equipment. Nothing else matters when you're soaring through the air, your humans watching in disbelief as you dive off the top of the fridge. You just need faith. And if you do miss your target, you'll automatically land on your feet; just check that you don't have buttered toast strapped to your back as it may affect your fall.

When you're ready to jump, let those pupils dilate and butt wiggle as you rocket yourself through the catmosphere. Let me know as soon as you're hanging out with the dust bunnies on top of the wardrobe.

I'm a surfer
So alert!
By the way
I'm on your shirt

28

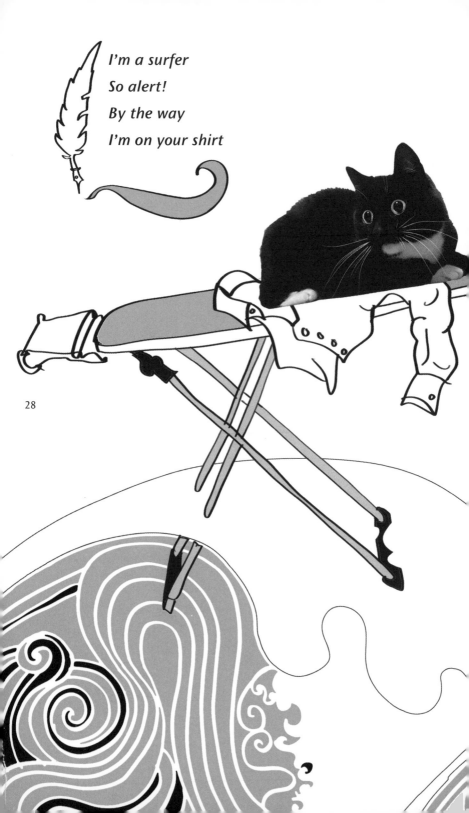

Ironing board surfing

The best things in life are often the most dangerous, and ironing board surfing is about as extreme as it gets. Demanding expert precision and balance, it is a gruelling sport that only the most daring cats practise. Timing is key, as you will need to wait patiently for your human to set up your surfboard. This could take days, weeks, or even months depending on the type of human you own.

Seasoned surfers insist it's not for the faint hearted, as few cats ever make it on board. Seize the moment, and you'll be rewarded with some of the most spectacular views over your kingdom. Steady yourself on the unpredictable sea of clothes as you ride the waves of complaints from your humans; an ideal way for them to let off steam. Your endurance will be tested to the limit as you battle it out with their levels of patience.

For more information about your surf schedule, consult your nearest clothes horse.

. . . AND FINALLY

Don't just stick to these five classic cat exercises, as you can practise a variety of other sports in your spare time. Most track and field events are easily adapted to the home or outdoors. Why not take part in the steeplechase around the kitchen counter tops, or attempt the high jump over a garden fence? Other sports may require additional equipment. If you're looking to get into Dressage or Shot Putt, check first to ensure you have a suitable litter tray.

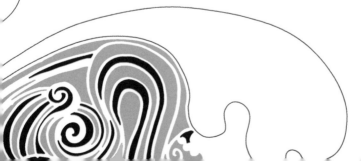

Dear diary

Sit, faceplant, inhale and leave. Twice a day. Same place, same bowl. Ever since recruiting my humans, I have become reliant on them for these so-called *meals*. As much as these brief interludes have kept me going, I find myself getting dangerously peckish during the periods in between.

It is never long before a craving strikes and I'm reduced to scavenging for scraps. I will admit that I supplement my diet with a variety of bugs, flies, plants and random debris around the house. There's also the occasional buffet on at the food bin (the chicken bones are a real hit!), but only if I can get past security. Without these options, I would get frustrated and desperate, heightening the risk of a stomach rumble. Unless I take matters into my own paws, I'm extremely concerned that it will become a more regular occurrence.

I have become increasingly curious about fending for myself in a more substantial way. After all, insects are unpredictable, and the plants are looking a bit tired. I have started to consider more sustainable alternatives. *What about fish!?* yelped the voice in my head. I wondered if I could get some on the internet; I hear from the furry human that this is where you can find *anything* these days. After a bit of searching, I stumbled upon a website with an impressive selection. All I had to do was register an account and fill in a few details, and they're going to start matching me with suitable fish!

PlentyOfFish.com

CuriousZelda

I am Zelda the cat. Hunter of house flies and keeper of string. Easily startled. Fish advocate. Often caught staring.

I'm just dipping my paw in the water, looking for tasty fish. Can you satiate me?

 DATING

Golddigga

 Hello! I saw your profile and noticed you like fish. I think we'd get on swimmingly.

Hai fishy! I'm Zelda. You look like quite the catch. In fact, I'd say I'm bowled over.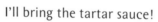

 Thank u! xoxo

How about dinner?

 For reel? Okay!

I'll bring the tartar sauce!

Hello?

Tina_Tuna

Hello Zelda. Wow, so you're a cat!
Are you looking for love?

What's love got to do with it?

Hahaha, I see what you did there.

?

So you wanna meet up some time?

I was thinking sushi!

Tina_Tuna has blocked you

Bubbly_goldfish

Hi, how are you!

Fine, and you?

Good thanks, how are you!

I said I'm fine.

WHOOPS sorry about that.

So how's it going?!?

CAREERS

I've made a ground-breaking discovery. As zany as it sounds, through my adventures I've found compelling evidence that there are other cats with whole other lives unfolding elsewhere. I know it's controversial, but I haven't stopped thinking about the adventures they may be having. What if there was a way to document them, and share their stories around the cat kingdom? Well, one thing led to another, and now I'm a News Anchor.

THE FUR O'CLOCK NEWS

Today's headlines:

CONFUSION IN THE BEDROOM as a curious organism was discovered under the duvet yesterday evening. Mr Foot is understood to have been attacked while working undercover on a slumber mission. He sustained minor injuries and was left shocked by the experience. 'It all happened so fast,' said Foot, in an exclusive interview with our mews team. The purrpetrator is yet to be identified, having fled the scene of the incident. Officials inform us that the search will continue under all sofas in the local area.

THE CHANCELLOR HAS ANNOUNCED changes to the budget in the houses of pawliament today. 'There will be CUTS! Delicious cuts of tuna for one and all!' cried the Chancellor while waving a piece of string. Pawliament had to be brought to order, as many cat MPs were awoken during the commotion.

Colonel Fluff, representing the Liberal Democats, told us, 'There was so much meowing it took ages to get back to sleep.' This measure substantially increases purrsonal Tuna allowances across the nation, and it will come into effect by dinner-time tomorrow.

COMING UP: could this be the world's most attractive Owl? A survey conducted by over twenty outdoor moggies placed Barney Twit at the top of a long list of head turners. We'll be live in his cave after the break.

NOW ONTO SPORT, and Fuzzy McLitter has broken the world record for the 2 metre curtain climb. The four-year-old Bengal, known for his agility on textiles, managed to reach the curtain rail in 3.4 seconds. Fur O'Clock News were unable to get hold of Fuzzy for an interview, as we are still waiting for him to climb down.

HUMANS AND FURNITURE

It may be a familiar scene for you: the humans have spent the past hour on your sofa, looking gormlessly at the television. They've laughed and gasped in equal measure. One of them even cried – or perhaps they *both* did, but the hairy one was trying desperately to hide it. You know they'll be stationed there for a while, as what began as 'sitting' soon became a 'slouch', and you expect they will soon be horizontal and drooling.

So why do they do it, and how could they look at a screen for so long? It's not exactly a moth on the wall, where literally *anything* could happen. My humans will in fact observe *other* humans who are pretending to be different humans altogether! Besides, who is Leonardo Di Catrio? I don't understand his movie, and he looks nothing like a wolf.

During these viewing sessions, the humans often beg for my company. They'll attempt a number of methods to coax me towards them, including:

- Speaking in a really high voice
- Making clicking or kissing sounds
- Frantically patting their thighs
- Covering themselves in cat biscuits
- Physically putting me on their laps

I applaud their determination, but why should I watch TV with them if they won't watch window with me?

I have made a decision to stick to watching my own shows thank you furry much, and encourage all cats to do the same. The storylines are far more stimulating, where the birds fly high and the squirrels chase each other around trees. Or a neighbour walks towards their car but goes back inside because they forgot something. You just can't write this stuff – it's the reason I subscribed to Petflix in the first place!

I believe we should instead be using the sofa for more practical things like slumber or clawing. I suppose I'll continue to allow my humans to sit on it, but the windowsill remains the best seat in the house.

HUMANS

My humans say that I'm aloof
They frequently complain
They are misled, to tell the truth
I feel I must explain

At times they call me from afar
They wish I was attentive
I find their actions quite bizarre
Because there's no incentive

'Zelda!' I can hear them shout
They call in desperation
'Nah,' I mutter to myself
I don't like confrontation

'Zelda?' they will ask again
While standing by the door
Quietly I count to ten
While staring at the floor

I watch them as they walk away
I did not interact
I live to lounge another day
My dignity intact

He had a bag
He wore a hat
He put some paper
On our mat

> Dear Zelda,
>
> What do mice taste of, and why do you eat them?
>
> Kind regards,
>
> Puzzled human

Dear inferior human,

If I had a housefly for every time someone asked me this, I would be very full indeed.

People often mistake mice for pests, which is alarming considering that they are a delicacy. Obviously, mice taste wonderful: succulent and savoury, rather like chicken. Sometimes nutty, with a faint aroma of cheese. Texture? Like eating a kiwi with the skin on.

I think the real question is, why don't *you* eat them? You don't need to go to a fancy restaurant to savour such delights. Wait until you are at home and as soon as you start to feel peckish, pull up all of your carpets and floorboards and wait for your mouse to appear. Catching one may take a while if you're one of those lazy humans who typically buys static food.

If you're not eating them by the time you've read my reply, you're missing out.

Best fishes,

Zelda

See a housefly
So discreet
Tiny war cry
Then I eat

Dear diary

The humans recently put up new photo frames. They think it complements my home and reminds them of nice times, but it has been a nightmare having to knock them all down again. My errands took longer than expected because they moved some of the existing frames, so I've had to rearrange them. All that, and I've still had to keep up with my furniture clawing.

I know I shouldn't overdo it, but I'm an adult cat now with many responsibilities. I get it from my mother. She could barely manage ten minutes of washing me without declaring, 'The sofa isn't going to scratch itself.' As much as I'd love to kick back all day in the airing cupboard, I have this nagging sense of duty to keep everything in meticulous order, and it's exhausting. I guess you could say it has been another stressful week.

With this in mind, I thought I would treat myself to a spa day. A chance to actually unwind and look after myself, for a change. No place for graft or endeavour. I mean, I wouldn't rule out destroying a cushion or two if the opportunity arose, but the aim of the day is to relax. 'Aren't spa days expensive!?' I hear you cry. Luckily, I found a really good deal, as this one was local and totally free of charge.

As soon as I entered the spa, I was greeted by a curiously prickly implement slowly floating towards me. Before I could begin my inspection, it swooped down onto my head, down my neck and along my back. It repeated these slow, sweeping strokes a number of times. I had a few reservations because the massage was relentless – heaps of fur were emerging around me, I thought I was having kittens! It was, however, doing wonders for my coat, and I felt fabulous.

My session came to an abrupt end as I realised I needed
to get to my facial. I strolled into the treatment room
and jumped onto the counter top. It was obviously a very
posh spa, as I noticed they had already prepared all of the
cucumber slices for me. There was also a bit of lettuce and
tomato to the side, which confused me. I wasn't sure what
to do, so I knocked it all onto the floor. It was a wonderful
facial and I felt very refreshed indeed.

As I padded around the spa looking for my next fix, I
encountered the most terrifying fog. Gingerly making my
way through the mist, I was meowtified to see a member
of staff dressed in just a towel. It soon dawned on me
that I was in the steam room; finally, somewhere I could
sit around and do nothing for a while. I had been warned
not to stay in there for long, I imagine due to the lack of
food, although the hot vapour was great for releasing the
impurrities from my paws.

Much as I tried to ignore them, the towel-clad staff
member had become intrusive, and so I decided to leave.
On my way out, I noticed that they had a Jacuzzi in the
corner! Sadly, they'd left the lid down. It would have been
ideal as I was already undressed.

It had been a long and invigorating day, but I sensed
something was missing. A feeling of being peckish
had gradually snuck up on me, and I was in danger of
encountering full-blown hunger. Luckily, they had included
a bonus one-course meal in the deal. I made my way to the
dining area and waited by the placemat with my name on
it (the attention to detail was more than adequate). The
waiter gently placed my food in front of me . . . Salmon
Pate in Jelly! My favourite! Coincidentally I'd had the same
meal that very morning, but it was just as fantastic, and
easily the highlight of my visit. Overall, I'm really pleased
that I went ahead with the spa day, and chose this one in
particular. It felt just like home.

ADVICE
FOR
CATS

HOW TO BEG IN THREE EASY STEPS

STARE IN SILENCE

The silent treatment is a surprisingly effective tool, using reverse psychology to trick your human into sharing their food with you. Watching quietly as they tuck into their meal will surely invoke feelings of guilt, and should inspire them to take pity on you. This method seldom gets instant rewards, so exercise patience; your chances of receiving a morsel improve with every passing second.

If particularly miserly, place yourself directly in front of your human(s), ensuring that you are clearly visible throughout the duration of the meal. Maintain eye contact at all times, and let your innate sense of longing and desperation radiate from you. Pro tip: never blink.

Be vocal

If the silent treatment isn't working, it's time to create some noise. Meowing usually gets you noticed, but it tends to lack conviction. Howling is a far more effective way to communicate your suffering and deprivation. When you're ready, throw your head back and open your mouth as wide as you can, letting as much sound spill out for as long as possible. Try to time your bellows just before your human takes each bite. Go high-pitched for urgency, or choose a lower register for a more sorrowful guilt trip. Ultimately howling is a skill that you need to practise regularly. For minimal background noise, stick to rehearsing during The Night.

Make contact

If you have already tried silence and vocalisation without success, you'll need a more direct approach. All it takes is a dash of physical contact and your belly should soon begin filling up. The secret is to stop food entering your human's mouth. Start by getting as close as you can to their face; anything up to an arm's length will do. If you're feeling confident, why not climb your human and perch on their shoulder? Once you're in position, wait for a forkful of food to arrive and swipe it away. There are few greater joys in life than seeing a chunk of chicken plummet to the kitchen floor. Go get it fur pal – you earned it!

Next to me my human sat
He looked at me in awe
Following our friendly chat
I struck him with my paw

DATING

HolySardine

 Good day Zelda, how are you?

Is it day already!?!

What are you doing awake?

 Just back from my morning worship. Church was packed!

Sounds enticing. Tell me more!

 Oh you make me blush. I'm just a caring, genuine, cod-fearing sardine.

Yummy! So, your plate or mine?

 What are you trying to say?

Dear diary

I'm not having much luck on *PlentyOfFish.com*. I seem to be doing a lot of chatting with other fish, but haven't managed to eat a single one. They're usually pleased to hear from me, but the conversations end earlier than expected.

It's hard trawling through profiles on an empty stomach, but perhaps I need to cast my net a bit wider. I'm not fussy about the type of fish I eat. As my humans well know I'll try anything once – even crab at a pinch.

AGONY AUNT

Dear Zelda,

I'm contacting you about a sensitive subject: diet and exercise. I've noticed my staff have been putting on a lot of weight recently. How can I save them?

Yours,

Mr. Buttons

Dear Mr. Buttons,

Excessive weight gain in a member of staff is a serious concern and must be addressed promptly. I can strongly recommend a personal trainer.

I speak from experience. About a year ago, a member of my staff put on a lot of weight. She was in good spirits at first, but as the pounds piled on she barely slept or left the house. Things came to a head during The Night, when she woke up in a panic and was taken away by ambulance.

When she returned home several days later, she had lost nearly all the weight! She was accompanied by her new personal trainer – a much smaller human called Peanut. He spends most of his time sleeping in a special basket and sticks to a high-protein milk-only diet. He does have a temper, but as he is getting results I don't question his methods.

If I were in your paws I would find your humans a personal trainer of their own immediately. The screaming and tail-pulling are a small price to pay for the long-term good health of your staff.

Best fishes,

Zelda

Just lost my job as a P.E. teacher
My pupils got too big

ZELDA THE HANDYCAT

Having mastered the culinary arts, I've felt that I could be doing more with my career. That's not to say that I haven't enjoyed my time on the kitchen worktops – I've just got bigger fish to fry.

Are cats good at home improvements? It's a question that many have asked over time, yet few cats have answered. It has always bugged me that labourers tend to be humans rather than cats – a curious anomaly considering the gulf in ability.

Is a thumb so important? Sure, there have been rare occasions when I *may* have benefited from having one; like picking something up. But apart from that, I see few reasons to employ a human without considering a cat first. Intrigued to put things right, I started my career in home improvements.

Coincidentally, my first day on the job was in my own home, where a number of important fixes were required.

JOB #1: PLUMBING

I noticed that my client's tap had been dripping since she last used it. Curious as to why this was happening, I thought I should investigate. I positioned myself on the rim of the sink to get a better view of the fault. As I moved my head closer to the spout, I tested the frequency of drips on my tongue. It was indeed a consistent drip and unfortunately beyond repair.

Job #2: Decorating

My client then led me into the bedroom and explained a common problem: 'Zelda, I've just changed the sheets.' It was a classic scenario of a customer attempting DIY without the necessary skills, and the result was disappointing. Following my thorough inspection, it was evident that the room required refurbishment. I proceeded to perform a series of rolls in various parts of the room, successfully coating every surface in a new layer of fur.

Despite my best efforts, my client seemed ungrateful.

Job #3: Plastering

Widely regarded as a tough craft to master, many cats shy away from plastering. It's a discipline requiring immaculate paw work and a unique set of tools in order to create a professionally smooth finish; no less than my client expected. I spent a while assessing all of the walls in the house in fine detail over the course of the day. I discovered that they were all flat and positioned vertically. I concluded that no plastering was required, much to the surprise of my client. She questioned my methods, repeatedly asking, 'Why are you still staring at that wall?'.

Not everyone values the efforts we cats invest in our property surveys.

Job #4: Electrical rewiring

Just when I thought my work was complete, I noticed an additional electrical issue. My client had failed the pat test. I hurried over to the TV stand, where I found a huge cluster of cables. As I began to strip them with my wire cutters, my client warned me to keep a safe distance. Luckily I knew what I was doing. After some rapid charging around the living room, I was satisfied that the circuit was complete.

Once I had finished for the day, I could tell that my client was relieved. After all, she'd chosen me because the previous builders weren't up to scratch. In fact, she was so happy with my workmanship that she suggested I stay for dinner, which I accepted. I'm confident that as long as I remain local and competitive, she'll hire me again.

CLOSE TO MY HEART

No eyes. No nose.
No thighs. No toes.
No feet. No head.
No seat. No bed.
No food. No budge.
No mood. No grudge.

  – 'Wall'

Dry face. Hard skin.
Wide base. No chin.
No sheen. No rust.
So clean. Then dust.

  – 'Skirting Board'

Green hands. Brown arms.
So still. Such calms.
One base. No feet.
No chase. Just eat.

  – 'Fern'

Scratch the sofa
Claw the bed
Tear the curtain
Still get fed

TOP ITEMS FOR CLAWING

THE SOFA

A classic scratching vessel. Stretch out and sink your claws into its side, or climb it and start kneading! Keep going until you see threads or hear your humans scream. Choose fabric for comfort or upgrade to leather for a more sophisticated level of damage.

CARPET

An ocean of clawing potential! Lie on your front and shred away, or stretch out on your side and yank those fibres with all your might. If interrupted, you can simply find another spot. Remember to watch out for those carpet grips.

TABLE LEGS

After consultation with a colony of beavers, I was informed that there is nothing quite as satisfying as hacking away at wood. I must say I was sceptical at first, but I've been surprised by the effectiveness of the results. Rather than hunting down a tree, you can fulfil your carpentry desires from the comfort of your home. The table leg is the perfect height for you to stretch out fully and start chipping away. Go with swift downward strokes to make it through the varnish, then lock in and scrape away, hanging your full bodyweight off your paws. Timber!

LAPS

Like them or loathe them, laps provide a supportive, heated surface, ideal for winter clawing. Available in a range of fabrics, this meaty hot water bottle offers satisfaction and unpredictability in equal measure. You'll face stiff competition for space as you bid to outsmart the laptop or TV-dinner tray. Once you've claimed your rightful space, switch to purring mode and dig into that dressing gown. Try to imagine that you're a furry baker kneading a couple of baguettes. How hard can you scratch? The thigh's the limit!

SCRATCH POST

The most elusive piece of furniture in the home. Many cats spend entire lifetimes searching for this curious object without success. Legend has it that you can claw one for an unlimited amount of time and never be criticised by your human . . . Many humans say that they are able to sense its mystical presence in the room, and some have even been seen pointing or ushering their cat to its imagined location – spooky!

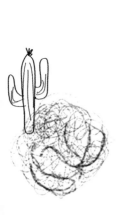

AGONY AUNT

Dear Zelda,

My servant is making strange noises. I think she is trying to touch her toes, but she's quite far off at the moment. Can you advise how to handle such behaviour?

Lots of glove,

Mittens

Dear Mittens,

60

This is very serious indeed. I had planned to destroy a cushion this afternoon, but after reading your letter, I thought it best to reply immediately.

I believe that the activity you are observing is 'yoga'. I've noticed that my humans also struggle to reach beyond their kneecaps. I've had to put many a shower on hold just to demonstrate the various movements.

With regard to your servant, all they need is a bit of physical intervention. When you notice them start their bend, jump up on their back and remain perfectly still – steady yourself using your claws if necessary. Listen out for any shouts or groans. The pain shows it's working.

With patience and purrseverence, you should eventually see them touching their shins.

Best fishes,

Zelda

SingleCrab

 HELLO, HOW ARE YOU?

 Sorry, crabs lock was on. Lol.

 Hello?

Musselman

 Hey Zelda, what's up?

Just in between naps. You?

 Just been at the gym

Steam room? 61

 Nah, working my abs. People try to crack you open, but you gotta stay strong. Do you work out?

I try to get to the scratching post when I can, but it's more convenient to just claw the couch.

 I get you.

Hang on, how are you even typing?

 Voice recognition. So, dinner sometime?

Yes! What are your thoughts on garlic and white wine?

Hello?

CAREERS

THE FUR O'CLOCK NEWS

Today's headlines:

SCIENTISTS HAVE DISCOVERED a genetic link between house cats and hermit crabs. The research carried out by the Bio Illogical Centre found that both species were prone to sitting around doing very little for long periods of time. The curious creatures were observed for a number of days in the same laboratory; a study described by one Behavioural Analyst as 'quite dangerous'. Dr Deathwish commented, 'What I found fascinating was their ability to sleep or remain inactive for up to 23 hours a day. For the remaining hour, both cats and hermit crabs used their claws a lot,' added Deathwish, who was unable to hold a microphone due to the bandages on his hands.

A NAVY-BLUE SOCK HAS BEEN CAUGHT illegally attempting to enter a light clothes wash. Nearby humans were quick to report the criminal, who has since been placed under a vest. Our legal correspondent briefly interviewed the offender as she was escorted to the Laundry Correctional Facility. Miss Polly Esther told Fur O'Clock News, 'I feel like I've been hung out to dry.'

A HIP NEW CONCEPT RESTAURANT opened today in the capital. Hordes of street cats gathered outside 'The Wheely Bin', described by its creative team as London's first flip-up restaurant, for its soft launch. The 'Bin, as millennials are already calling it, has been an instant hit. We spoke to Head Chef Robin Garbàge, a chartreux, who lifted the lid on his latest project: 'The Wheely Bin has really been a success. All our ingredients are hyper local and the menu changes by the day, depending on what comes in. Which is also why we're closed on Thursdays.'

Social media was abuzz, with the restaurant's trashtag trending on Instagram within hours. User DalstonTabster claimed that dessert was 'still relatively fresh' and 'hard to refuse'; a post that already has thousands of mews. Today's launch marks a growing trend towards leftover-fusion cuisine, as chefs across London incorporate street food into their menus. Garbàge plans to roll out the concept more widely in the coming months. And with thousands of potential locations to choose from across the city, there could soon be a Wheely Bin on every corner.

BREAKING NEWS:
A GLASS ORNAMENT

Spiders

Squirrels

Houseflies

HOOVER

64

MICE

ZELDA

HUNTING &
NATURAL SELECTION

HUMAN'S DINNER

FOOD BIN

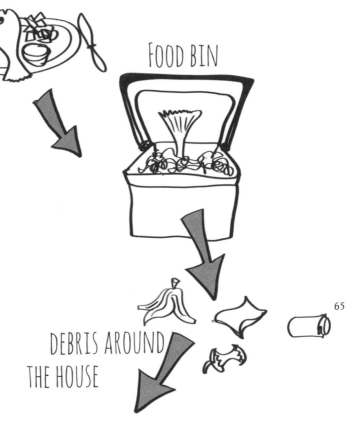

65

DEBRIS AROUND
THE HOUSE

WET FOOD

DRY FOOD

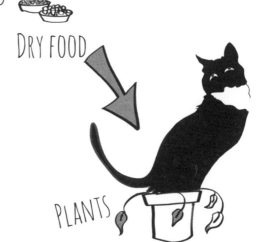

PLANTS

TOP HUNTING TARGETS

HOUSEFLIES

Formerly known as cave flies, these brave bonbons don't care about your privacy. Leave a window open and they'll enter your home unannounced, ready to conduct a full property survey. They'll hurry from room to room, landing on each of your belongings until their next appointment. That is, of course, unless you're feeling peckish.

As houseflies are physically incapable of flying in a straight line, few other targets require as much skill as a hunter. It may take a few attempts before you manage to catch one, but try not to be disheartened. Chances are they'll be sticking around for a while, as they generally struggle to find the window they entered through. Also, keep in mind that the toughest targets are the most rewarding, and these winged raisins are as juicy as they come.

Every so often you'll get lucky and find one sleeping on your windowsill, but your typical housefly hunt demands speed and dexterity. Soon as you encounter one, follow my easy step-by-step guide to make sure you don't miss out.

1. Crouch down into the *I'm about to jump* position
2. Wait for a fly to pass over your head
3. Jump as high as you can and take a wild swipe

Repeat this process until you feel a tingling sensation between your paws.

Quickly transfer the fly to your mouth, but don't start chewing yet! You'll not only get a buzz, but also a free electric toothbrush.

Squirrels

These anxious appetisers aren't everyone's cup of flea, as they're particularly awkward to fit through a cat flap. They also tend to live in trees, which can make things complicated, especially if you live in the desert. If you're the type of cat who likes their dinner served chilled and in jelly, this prey really isn't for you.

But if you're determined enough, I've found a really clever trick to catching them. It took me months of research, calculations and practice, but I've finally cracked it. First, check that you are not indoors. Then, lower yourself until you are completely flush with the ground. Next, wiggle your butt exactly fourteen times. Finally, run as fast as you can in the exact direction of the squirrel. This can take some time if the squirrel is far away.

Your reward is a gamey, somewhat nutty meal that even comes with its own bushy carrying handle. And if you can't finish a whole one, why not share the rest with your human?

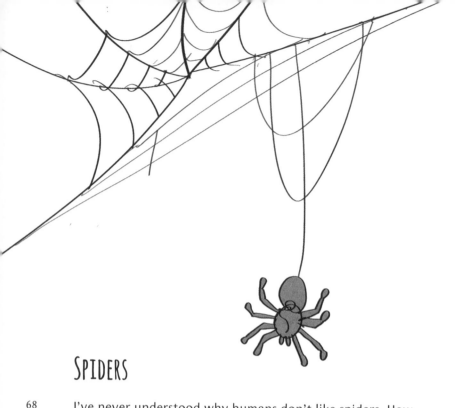

Spiders

I've never understood why humans don't like spiders. How could anyone *not* be impressed by something that can walk on ceilings and build butt nets? I sense the humans are scared of them, as they can only flap their arms in terror whenever they encounter one. But honestly, spiders are actually really friendly once you get to eat them.

It's a good thing they're such a convenient snack. They're low calorie and require minimal preparation. You can get overly fussy – carefully removing each leg, crisping them up gently in a sun puddle. Personally, I like to eat them straight out of the bathtub.

MICE

Irresistible, frantic, furry profiteroles. The appearance and movement of a mouse triggers our natural hunting instinct like no other prey. According to science, their tails have evolved to look more and more like a piece of string. They aren't always easy to catch, as these busy goujons insist on scuttling quickly in every direction other than towards our mouths. It's also problematic that they spend most of their time in places we can't get to, possessing the ability to fit through the tiniest gaps (*even* tighter than the sock drawer).

It's no surprise that we don't get them in cat food. Despite high demand for tinned mice, humans can't figure out how to catch them. As we cannot rely on such hopeless hunters, you'll have to source them yourself. Before you begin, make sure that you are able to correctly identify a mouse. For your convenience, I've put together this helpful diagram:

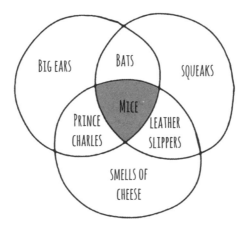

Soon as you spot one, let go of any inhibitions and dignity, and let nature take its course. If you've done it correctly, you should find yourself fervently courting said mouse until it lies somewhere between claw and fang. Also, don't be afraid to play with the mouse before the kill. Granted, it's slightly torturous for them, but who could blame you when you've been brought up hunting catnip toys?

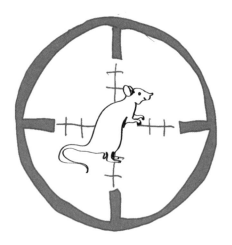

RED DOT

Unlike rodents or houseflies, Red Dot is yet to be defeated. She can move at incredible speed and disappear at will, surviving countless battles unscathed. She effortlessly breaches my security measures, breaking into our home and then dancing on the floors or hanging off the ceiling as she pleases. She'll taunt me by moving slowly when I'm far away, and then speeding off up a wall just as I'm about to pounce.

Her motives are unclear, and all attempts to uncover them have been met with laughter, usually from my humans. Of course, those poor, simple creatures are blissfully unaware of the mortal danger posed by such a capable foe. She appears to be targeting humans, only emerging from the shadows when they're around. While there have been no reported attacks on humans, many cats have sustained injuries during high-speed chases.

My humans try to be supportive, remarking 'Maybe next time, Zelda!' What they don't know is that I've been practising my stalking on household ornaments all week. Can you imagine the glory when *we* finally capture Red Dot? I was so very close once. But then I lost her behind the magazine rack.

TAIL

Will it swing left? Will it swing right? Who knows what Tail is going to do next. I'm curious to find out, having put a lot of time and effort into chasing it, but it feels like we're just going around in circles. It appears that the harder I try, the harder it is to get hold of. I applaud any cat who manages to grab it. I'm resigned to the idea that I may never actually catch Tail, and I suppose I'll just have to put it behind me.

Had an inkling
Had a hunch
Saw a squirrel
That was lunch

 DATING

Krill_Sergeant

 WHO ARE YOU! YOU HAVE 5 SECONDS
TO ANSWER!

Woah. I'm Zelda.

 WHERE DO YOU LIVE?

 I SAID WHERE DO YOU LIVE!

London. What do you want!?

  ATTENTION!

 WHY ARE YOU ON HERE!

 I'm looking for my partner in brine

 YOU THINK THIS IS A JOKE!?

You need to take a krill pill

 DISMISSED!

Eager_Amoeba

 Hi Zelda. I read your ad. You seem really complex and interesting!

Thanks. Why is your profile so empty?

Don't read too much into it. I'm young, free and single cell!

hahaha

Huh?

Dear healthcare professional,

I'm concerned about the mental state of our shoe rack. He's been acting very strangely lately. I can't quite put my paw on it, but he's just not himself. We used to be able to talk for hours. We'd share all of our secrets, and sing at the top of our lungs together during the night. I used to nap on top of him and he would always remain still so as not to wake me.

However, when I'm lying on top of him lately, I feel uncomfortable. He's been steadily collecting more and more shoes over time. They used to be neatly stacked in pairs, all facing forwards. Nowadays, they're flung all over the place, with all shoes great and small pressed against one another. Flip flops balancing on hiking boots. Trainers hanging by a shoelace. Just yesterday I found a knee-length boot slumped across the top shelf!

It's affecting my humans too. When the shoe rack first moved in, they would constantly go on about how much they loved it: how it was such a useful addition to the home; how it fitted so perfectly in its space; how there was 'much more room in the hallway now, dear'. Now, when they're rummaging around for their footwear, it's clear the magic has gone.

It's the shelf-neglect that worries me most. The shoe rack has supported me on many levels, and so I feel it's my duty to intervene. With your help, I'm hopeful the situation can be re-paired.

Anxiously yours,

Zelda

Dear diary

I've recently noticed that the day is split into two very distinct parts. One is a time for rest, recovery and tranquillity. The other is commonly referred to as The Night.

My recollection of the former is hazy. With my humans absent for most of it, I am somehow less motivated to trash the place. I instead find myself frequently slipping in and out of consciousness between meal times, chain-snoozing from one item of furniture to the next. I can't seem to shake the habit, as my sleepy expeditions mysteriously transport me from the carpet to the back of the sofa, under the piano stool, atop the wardrobe and into the sock drawer. I know my action-packed lifestyle isn't for everyone, but beauty sleep is as important as it is exhausting.

The Night is a curiously different kettle of tuna, as the humans disembark from my sofa and head upstairs to my bed. Here they remain in vaguely horizontal heaps until the light returns. Having observed them over time, they seem to be very casual about the time they go to lie down, but really strict about the time they get up.

When they want to go to sleep, they insist on turning off all of the lights. It's highly inconvenient, as The Night is the ideal time for me to get things done. How can I complete my activities if I'm struggling to see where I'm going? It is only natural that I knock things over. And between you and me, have you ever tried to use a litter tray in complete darkness?

Their behaviour during The Night concerns me deeply. I don't mind the odd disturbance, but it's very distracting when you hear two sets of heavy breathing vibrating throughout the house. I cannot comprehend how they sleep through such raucous, nasal thunder. Are they actually sleeping? Or are they secretly herding pigs? I wouldn't be surprised, with the amount of movement I hear from the other side of the door. I expect *some* rustling in pursuit of optimum comfort, but I can barely eat a potted plant without hearing some kind of activity. At times, they will independently get up and leave their enclosure; I watch in horror as they have the audacity to urinate in my Jacuzzi!

On rare occasions, their movement is so deliberate and persistent that I am convinced it must be happening during waking moments. And I think we all know *exactly* what they're doing. Is it *really* appropriate for them to be practising yoga in the dark?

Towards the end of The Night, the light gradually creeps into my home and the beak band begins. I listen intently as they serenade me from all directions. 'Play the one about the worms!' I howl, engrossed in the ongoing jam session. Their set is however routinely interrupted by a piercing siren from the bedroom. It sounds for a short time and then ends abruptly. I hear nothing for a while until it restarts. This process mysteriously repeats several times until I finally hear my humans grunting to each other. Why do they subject themselves to this ritual? How can they function with such little sleep?

I force the door open and rush to their aid, leaping onto the bed to help unearth them from the duvet. 'Good morning Zelda,' they croak. While they slowly get up, I race around the room, covering every fibre of carpet to ensure that everything is in its rightful place. They eventually stumble out of the room to a sea of debris as they discover newly broken ornaments and fallen photo frames. It could have been avoided of course, if only they had left a lamp on for me.

The first rule of night club is:
You do not talk about night club.

12 HOURS OF DARKNESS

Due to the many mysterious goings-on during The Night, I decided to record my findings during 12 hours of darkness.

7PM

The drawer opens and she reaches in. She pulls out her weapon and holds it aloft. She issues a menacing cry, 'ZELLLDDAAAAAAA!!!!!.' I'm already there. My fate lies with her, and I know this won't take long. Amid a deafening chorus of bangs and scrapes, I notice she's on edge. Her preparation is swift. She looks over to me, sporting a devilish grin. We lock eyes, and she makes her approach. With a final slap of her slipper on the linoleum, she's standing over me. It's actually happening. She bends down slowly, and with a full extension of the arm, delivers the kill. It's roast chicken, and it tastes sublime.

7.15PM

I realise that I may have concluded dinner prematurely, and there may in fact be fragments of chicken remaining in and around my bowl. I return to my eating station, searching for second helpings. My findings are limited, but

7.30PM

In the spirit of completeness, I return to my eating station for a final sweep. No traces found.

7.35PM

I notice that my scent isn't right. It's time for a shower, and this one's a full body wash.

8PM

A moth has entered my home and I must observe it. Cancel all my appointments, for I now have an entirely new purpose in life. He looks peaceful.

8.05PM

He was saltier than expected.

9PM

A feeling of lethargy strikes, and I enter my final snooze of the day. Luckily, I am already positioned in the doorway. I

10.50PM

I'm awake! I'm also ready to spend some quality time with my staff. I patrol their laps, nuzzling them as I go along. Holy shrimp, I'm purring. Awkward!

11PM

The humans are going to bed. I race ahead of them and wait, attempting to clutch their ankles while they hurdle me in the hallway. They instead seem intent on giving me a belly rub. I know they're just buttering me up before lockdown. The massage ends sooner than expected, as they barely cover each nipple before serving me my notice. 'Night night Zelda.'

The light disappears and the bedroom door closes behind them.

11.01PM

The house is clear! It's the perfect opportunity to brush up on my circuit training!

12AM

I sing my humans a soothing lullaby and wish them a restful sleep. They'll need it in order to fulfil their duties after The Night.

1AM

During my stroll around the living room, I experience congestion at the bookshelf. I weave my way through the various obstacles in my path, some crashing to the floor. Lighting conditions are poor, so I will review the situation

1.45AM

I'm ready for my stakeout. I look out across a dusky field, methodically examining the area from my windowsill. I remain perfectly still; just one accidental movement and I risk blowing my cover. I need to be prepared, for I know it could appear at any moment. That is, once I figure out what I'm looking for.

2.30AM

I simply must lick my foot. Upon closer inspection, I decide to give myself a deep clean, hoovering up everything lodged between my toes.

3AM

I notice another cat outside looking directly at me. After a brief staring contest, he begins to sing a familiar melody. It's the song of my people! I throw my head back and proudly howl along with him at the top of my lungs. I realise that I may never socialise with him, but for just half

3.45AM

Something isn't right. I'm feeling nauseous. I try to steady myself, my paws pressed firmly into the carpet. My head is heavy and I'm precariously hunched over. A momentary twitch escalates to a tremble, and I'm shivering. My heart thrashes against my chest, my face numb. I rock back and forth uncontrollably as I enter full body convulsion. My nose itches. My whiskers quiver. My ears flutter. And a hairball is born.

4AM

I'm getting a bit peckish. I don't want to ruin my breakfast, so I opt for salad. The selection isn't great, but the trusty fern hits the spot.

4.15AM

I am exhausted. I have no idea what has come over me, but I'm desperate for a nap. I don't think I can make it any further until I get some rest. The kitchen counter will have to suffice.

5AM

Look who just came swanning in! It's none other than my tail! I must see to this immediately.

5.30AM

Not sure if I cleaned the top of my head earlier. Better safe than sorry.

6AM

The feathered musicians have arrived! The brave soloist flaps up to the stage and her beak opens for the intro. With some hesitation, the choir gradually joins in, building to a glorious chorus of chirrups. The sound is chaotic and yet peaceful. I would eat them but they're actually really talented.

6.30AM

MAYDAY! The alarm makes me panic, and I attempt to claw my way under the bedroom door. Just as I'm about to squeeze through, the door opens.

6.35AM

The humans are in my bed and appear inactive. I dive on top of them, frantically biffing their faces to help them regain consciousness. I detect suspicious movement under the duvet — someone attacking a member of staff! I leap to their aid, managing to quell the assailant. 'OUCH!' yells my human. If only they realise that I've saved them from peril — it could have been so much worse.

7AM

Predictably, my team are late for work. I wait patiently at my eating station, occasionally marching in a tight circle to pass the time — I always get anxious before my breakfast meetings. When the waiter eventually arrives, he procrastinates, refilling my water bowl and making idle conversation. I find him intrusive as he repeatedly questions my behaviour. I relent, screaming back at him, '*I'M* A GOOD GIRL!' Finally, my meal is served and I wedge my face into the bowl and just like that, The Night is

My humans say
They need a rest
They disappear
I'm not impressed

I scurry over
Head hung low
Will I make it?
Will they know?

But when they sleep
I must confess
I feel inspired
To make a mess

Tension growing
Feet unsteady
Teeth are showing
Claws are ready

The house is still
The house is dark
The time has come
To make my mark

In position
Scratch away!
Fabric pulling
Starts to fray

The coast is clear
The room is free
No humans near
It's all for me

What a rush!
What a blast!
Must stay hush
Must be fast

I spot the couch
I plan my move
And I can vouch
They won't approve

Sorry sofa
Damage done
Mission over
That was fun

I am Zelda, I am the night
By the way my bib is white

 DATING

Crusty42

 Hey Zelda, what are you up to?

I'm just sitting in the hallway. You?

 Not much. Chilling in the Atlantic.

Sorry about my photo by the way. I'm much better in reel life.

Don't apologise. I think you look tasty ;)

Thanks. I'm really intrigued by your profile. I've always wondered what life is like above sea level.

Mostly dry.

 Hahah. You're a witty kitty.

 Fancy meeting up sometime?

 ?

Dear diary

I actually enjoyed chatting with Crusty. It's strange, as I've never really thought of an appetiser in this way. I must have eaten hundreds of prawns without much regard for their character, but with Crusty, it's different. He seemed genuinely interested in getting to know me.

Being friends with your prey is ridiculous of course. However, even though I'm starving as I write, I just can't imagine eating him. It would be shellfish. I'm not saying he wouldn't be delicious, but I almost think I'd miss him afterwards.

Thinking about it, I've never really had a close friend.

My humans do make an effort, but I prefer to keep things professional with my staff. There's little time to stop and chat with mice and houseflies, and my conversations with the pot plants feel one-sided. I have tried getting closer to the shoe rack, but we're still not on speaking terms. And before you ask, I hardly know any of the cats in my neighbourhood. What am I supposed to do? Just walk up to one and lick their face – like they're my mother?

All I know for sure is that with Crusty I felt a connection. I'm curious about that.

CLOSE TO MY HEART

No lips. No head.
No hips. No thread.
So shine. No grips.
No sign. I slips.

   – Window sill

One head. One foot.
No bed. Stay put.
One place. One bag.
No face. No brag.

   – Pedal Bin

93

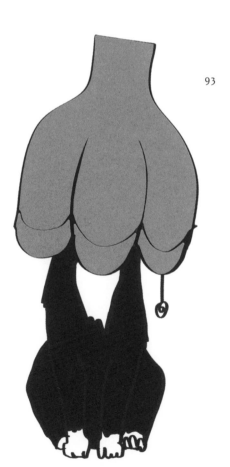

No face. No bed.
High place. No fed.
So cone. Such shine.
Alone. Den mine.

   – Lampshade

HOW TO COPE WITH . . .

BABIES

Miracles of nature. Delicate, innocent, vulnerable, milk explosions waiting to happen. Experience the wrath of one's mother as she interprets your curious glances as a threat to her young. Be near one at your peril, as you cannot be trusted not to upset the baby. Cope by hiding in the laundry basket or moving to another planet.

CHILDREN

They may appear innocent, but make no mistake: these tipsy dwarfs are dangerous and unpredictable. Soon as they notice you, they will produce a high-pitched siren to signal their approach, as they stumble towards you with an outstretched, sticky hand. Make a dash for it, or they will grab you and never ever let go.

OTHER CATS

One's territory is sacred and must not be compromised by other cats venturing anywhere near it. I keep mine to a modest size, roughly that of our neighbourhood. Should another cat encroach, a tiny alarm goes off in my head. This triggers panic and sudden wide-eyed glances in their precise direction, often confused with 'staring at the wall'.

There is simply no reason for another cat to be within your minimum radial distance, unless they are siblings, or you are dating them, or both. Should you encounter an unauthorised cat, the only way to cope is by preparing for the worst possible outcome. First, cancel all of your meetings for the day as this will take priority. Next, arch your back and raise your hackles. Then, slowly open your mouth wide to bare your fangs and let out a raucous hiss; this will tell the offender that they are not welcome near you, or that you have something stuck in your throat. Finally, stare at the other cat until they break eye contact or the world ends.

Dogs

Why should I trust someone who eats their own poop? These inferior organisms can – and will – lick everything in their local area. Their hygiene standards are concerning. It seems perfectly normal for them to roll around in unidentified sticky, smelly substances. Rumour has it that some dogs are totally incapable of cleaning themselves, submitting to their humans for routine grooming; evidently a waste of such comically large tongues.

Crucially, dogs do not have any concept of personal space, so we need to teach them. If a dog approaches you, first arch your back and get your hackles up. Next, slowly raise a paw, as if to say, 'if you come any closer, I'll biff you.' Finally, biff them.

Elderly people

Less coping, more enjoying. Elderly people know what matters in life. You won't find them constantly rushing around doing errands or checking their smartphones. They appreciate living in the moment, at a more graceful pace, just like cats. They live life true to themselves, without inhibitions. Sure, they won't clean their butts before an audience like I would, but they're still impressively authentic humans and I would 100% sit on all of them.

Visitors

A 'Visitor' is the technical term for someone who isn't a member of staff, but desperately wants to be. From the moment one enters your home they are auditioning for your approval. During the interview, it is completely normal for a Visitor to put you on edge, as they will have typically interrupted something important you were doing. They will often be too loud, too quiet or too moderate. Some will carry hauntingly pungent smells, interfering with the scent markings you've tirelessly planted around the house. Some will completely ignore you, while others will relate to you as if you are a dog. You can also count on each guest to address you at a curiously high pitch, as if you are unable to hear the frequencies of a normal human voice. Thankfully, with my rating system you'll know exactly how to cope with the variety of Visitors entering your home.

For each guest you encounter, choose a score between 1 and 10, where 1 is *Repulsive* and 10 is *Acceptable*.

Rating	What to do	Visitor
1/10	Scratch	
2/10	Growl at	Delivery people,
3/10	Hiss at	Salesmen, Cleaners
4/10	Hide from	
5/10	Watch from afar	
6/10	Approach, then run away	
7/10	Sniff hand, then run away	Friends & Family
8/10	Accept petting, then run away	
9/10	Accept petting, then stay nearby	
10/10	Cover in fur	Guests who dislike cats

If, however, you find that you regularly hiss, growl at or attack guests, you may need to consult a behaviourist. It will take time and patience, but they *should* be able to help your Visitors improve their conduct.

Dear diary

Rugs. I've been on them for as long as I can remember. My parents were into them, and I was brought up thinking that they were okay. But I've always known that rugs can be dangerous, especially the harder ones.

I remember my very first rug experience. My humans brought one home, all perfectly rolled up! I was so casual about it back then, using them just because they were available, and I didn't have much else to do. I was just a comfort user, doing it when nobody was looking. It all seemed harmless. After all, recreational rugs are okay in moderation. They not only inject life into a room, but also help you feel more relaxed by covering up your floors.

However, lately I can't seem to get enough, as I can barely go a few hours without being on one. The longer the sessions last, the harder it feels to stop, and I lose sight of all the things I have to do in a day. I feel ashamed to admit it, but I'm worried that I may have a rug addiction.

When you're on rugs, you're at your lowest. Everyone wants to know if you've been using them yet few admit it; it's much easier to lie. I've been on this one rug recently which has been so difficult to come off. I know I should stop, but I find myself craving a thicker and thicker pile.

I recently spent the whole day on a rug. I got so engrossed in it that I completely lost track of the time. Regrettably, it turns out that I had over-dozed. My humans cottoned on when they found me sprawled out on the floor, face down in a pool of my own kibble. I'm also hesitant to try the rug in the hallway again after it made me trip. I don't know how many more times I can slip up.

So, I'm trying to make some positive changes in my life. I actually spent most of yesterday evening in the bathroom to get away from it. I thought it would do me good, but after a night on the tiles I only craved it more. I've come to appreciate how difficult it is to kick the habit, especially when I'm exposed to those high-traffic areas. I just don't want my humans getting pulled into the gritty underbelly of the rug scene. Hopefully they'll know better – they've seen how long I've spent getting clean.

I didn't choose the rug life

The rug life chose me

CAREERS

ZELDA THE EXPLORER

Many of my adventures are spontaneous, without the need for strategy or planning. There are, however, more daunting expeditions where a professional approach is required. I've often been tempted to pursue a career in travel and visit the long list of places on my bucket. One thing led to another, and now I'm an Explorer.

I've always wanted to visit the North Pole, having grown up listening to stories of legendary cats who braved it. My grandfather would meow for minutes on end about his intrepid adventures; the weeks away from home, trotting across the barren landscape with limited sustenance. 'Tins of tuna were a lot heavier back then,' he would insist, as I lay on the carpet, eagerly chewing my foot.

I *have* had chances to go in the past, but I have been terrified of putting one of my lives at risk. Plus it's never easy to find space in my busy schedule. Just yesterday, I had arranged back-to-back naps in the afternoon, although they got cancelled as I couldn't find anyone to sleep back-to-back with. Besides, I have always lacked the essential gear for such a daring voyage.

But that changed. One morning I was napping in a chest of drawers, when I unexpectedly trod on something hard. Upon sniffing it, I realised that it was my grandfather's

compass! I could still see the claw marks! Carrying it
in my mouth, I scrambled out of the drawer and into
the hallway, where I stood for roughly twenty minutes,
promising that today would be different. 'My shower must
wait,' I muttered to myself. Without much more hesitation,
I said my farewells and headed North.

My trek through the carpeted lands highlighted the
importance of fitness. However much I'd trained, little
could have prepared me for the steep inclines I faced. The
physical exertion was intimidating. I admit I nearly gave
up over fears for my safety, halting my trip mid-way for
a crisis nap. But the thrill of exploring pushed me to go
further, and I eventually reached the summit. I trudged
ahead, the air uncomfortably cool against my cheeks. I
clambered onto an icy ledge. Visibility was low and the
conditions harsh, and before I could gather myself, I
slipped.

I experienced a rapid drop in altitude as I tumbled and
skidded onto a vast bed of snow. I had reached the icy
wilderness! White in every direction, just like the stories
promised. I was alone, but for the eerie echoes of my own
mews. The temperature was falling and I was regretting
wearing my summer coat. I struggled to get any kind of
grip on the terrain. There were no carpets, cushions or
throws here; just a blank canvas, a bit like my CV. Not
a meal nor morsel in sight. I anxiously reached for my
supplies, but soon realised that I didn't have any pockets.

I started to panic. I was stranded in an unclaimed territory,
devoid of foil balls and string. Who was looking after my
belongings in my absence? Did they have any idea about
the level of upkeep involved? Worrying was futile, and I
had to remain focused on survival.

My tail swept erratically from side to side, increasing in speed the more I watched it. Why was it so difficult to control? My heart was racing, beating so hard I could hear it. It sounded like a dripping tap. Just then, I spotted my human's face looming over the horizon.

'Zelda, what are you doing in the bathtub?'

The words of my grandfather came flooding back, as I recalled the song he used to sing as he licked me to sleep:

Beware, the North Pole, you should know
The challenge will be strong
Beware, the Plug Hole, when you go
And don't forget this song

AGONY AUNT

Dear Zelda,

I'm feeling concerned about the weather. Over the past few weeks, my sunbathing time has reduced sharply. The chilly air and boggy ground mean it's no longer pleasant to go outside either. So far I've been keeping my spirits up by re-ordering the sock drawer, but in my heart of hearts I know that won't keep me occupied for more than a month or two at best. What can be done?

Yours,

Lady McPaws

Dear Lady,

I was concerned too, so I asked my field research team to dig into this. They confirmed that the field is indeed very muddy, and they're working hard to get to the bottom of it. We'll have to wait to see what they unearth, but I strongly suspect the root cause here is what the humans call 'Winter'.

Thankfully, the humans have various ancient rituals with which to tackle it. First, they sacrifice a tree and decorate their home around it. They then chant and feast, exchanging socks and candles with one another to boost morale. This may all sound like primitive superstition to you, but somehow it works. After only a few weeks, I notice the days grow longer and the climate improves.

If your humans aren't taking action on their own, you can help. Find their special equipment (look for a box of shiny balls and ribbon, often on top of a wardrobe) and sweep it onto the floor. They might resent your intervention at first, but they'll soon be reminded of their duties and join you in taking action against Winter.

Best fishes,

Zelda

I showed my humans something
Which cannot be unseen
I hope it was inspiring
To know my butt was clean

106

ADVICE
FOR
CATS

HOW TO SHOW HUMANS YOU CARE

Bring them gifts

Everybody loves gifts, including your staff. The best ones are the big surprises, especially when it's something the receiver can't obtain themselves. Like a mouse. Have you ever seen a human catch one? Neither have I. Why not give them the five-star treatment and serve breakfast in bed? Fresh, locally sourced wildlife deposited on their pillow is guaranteed to elicit shrieks of excitement. Your staff may be too animated to thank you, but the look on their face makes it all worthwhile.

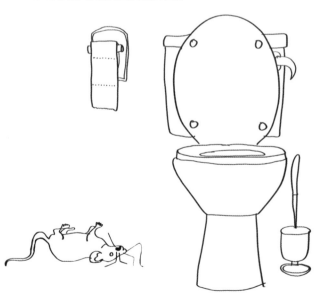

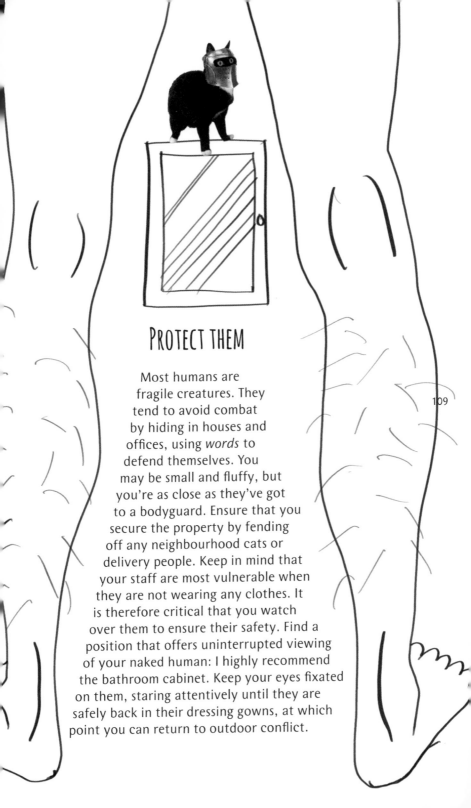

Protect them

Most humans are
fragile creatures. They
tend to avoid combat
by hiding in houses and
offices, using *words* to
defend themselves. You
may be small and fluffy, but
you're as close as they've got
to a bodyguard. Ensure that you
secure the property by fending
off any neighbourhood cats or
delivery people. Keep in mind that
your staff are most vulnerable when
they are not wearing any clothes. It
is therefore critical that you watch
over them to ensure their safety. Find a
position that offers uninterrupted viewing
of your naked human: I highly recommend
the bathroom cabinet. Keep your eyes fixated
on them, staring attentively until they are
safely back in their dressing gowns, at which
point you can return to outdoor conflict.

Help them declutter

Humans are hoarders. They collect numerous objects during their lifetimes, but barely interact with most. This is dangerous, as stationary items left unnoticed could attract dust bunnies to your home. Thankfully, you can deter them. 'Meow?' I hear you ask. I'll tell you how, by simply batting the ornaments onto the floor. In doing so, you'll draw your humans towards the fallen item, at which point they can re-evaluate whether they need it. Sometimes the decision is made for them if the ornament breaks; this can only be a good thing as it creates room on your windowsill for spying and meditation. Don't be discouraged if your staff appear resentful when gluing the pieces back together. By destroying their belongings you've helped them realise how much they value them. As I always say, *if it's worth mending, it's worth keeping.*

Keep them on schedule

A human's life will never be as busy as yours, but they may still have *some* commitments to fulfil. Help them get into a healthy routine by waking them at the start of their day. Aim to do so comfortably before the sun comes up. There are a number of methods, but I've found direct contact to be the most effective. Feel free to meow at them, but nothing says 'wake up' quite like a paw to the face. Get in position by jumping directly on top of them, and continue thumping them until they reach a vertical position. Whack-a-doodle-doo!

Clean them

Humans are all too relaxed about personal hygiene. On average, they wash themselves just *once* a day, and some don't even use their tongues. When your staff aren't presentable it reflects badly on you, and if they are unwilling to emulate your cleaning rituals, it's time to intervene. Wait for moments when they are calm, ideally on your sofa, and climb on their shoulders. Whip out your tongue and proceed to lick their forehead, covering their entire face until the saltiness subsides. Humans also tend to use artificial, fragranced products during the grooming process. Restore order by rubbing your face on them until they are completely covered in your natural scent. There. Good as new.

Dear diary

After a lot of sole searching, I've realised something. Seafood isn't my priority; truth be told I already *have* plenty of fish. It's *companionship* that I've been lacking. Although I clicked with Crusty, I had to let him down gently. It would never have worked. The long distance would have made things tricky, and I discovered he was obsessed with swimming. We're just very different genetically (although I don't mind a few curves).

What if I could find someone more like me? Someone who really appreciates the art of catching a housefly. Someone to go on long walks with around the kitchen, or to freak out with under the sofa. I've spent a lot of time thinking about this in the wardrobe. It might sound crazy, but maybe what I need in my life is . . . *another cat?*

The idea of meeting nose to nose feels daunting, but after a quick Zoogle search it turns out you can find more than just seafood online. I found an interesting site with lots of other cats looking to meet. With a dash of catnip courage, I signed up. They wanted me to create a profile. At first I was a bit hesitant to put my picture on the internet, but eventually I took the plunge.

Entwined

CuriousZelda

About me:

I'm mew to this, but here goes. I'm a curious, moderately anxious, furry lady. I'm very playful, and can easily while away an afternoon pawing at a ball of foil. I stay in shape with regular hunting, yoga, and randomly sprinting up and down stairs.

I like going out, often several times a day. Though sometimes it's nice to stay in and relax on top of the fridge. I'm an avid string collector and a big fan of upholstery. I also love animals, tinned or freshly caught.

I'm very private. I write poetry in my spare time – could you be my partner in rhyme?

Looking for:

I'm looking to meet someone kind and clawing. Someone who opens cat flaps for me. Someone to rub my face on.

You'll ideally be clean, with no matted fur and your own litter tray. Good mouser preferred. Timewasters welcome. Don't message me if you're not microchipped.

YOGA

Recently my human said
'I need to lose some weight'
I warned her of the road ahead
While staring at her plate

She said she'll try some exercise
It seemed her mind was set
I hinted that it wasn't wise
My lap time under threat

She said it would be calming
And give her peace of mind
She said it was the secret
To a peachier behind

She'll need a transformation
To make her stomach flat
She's logging onto Amazon
To buy a yoga mat

Her pants are tightly fitted
Like paint upon on her skin
She's finally committed
She's ready to begin

She's getting on her hands and knees
She does a downward dog
She holds it 'til her muscles seize
It's proving quite a slog

Suddenly she's very still
She's standing on one leg
She has the will but not the skill
She wobbles like an egg

Next she tries to touch her toes
Her T-shirt's riding higher
The sweat is pouring off her nose
I beg her to retire

She tries a salutation
But cannot hold it long
She asks for confirmation
Of what she's doing wrong

I'm on the bed observing
Admiring her persistence
I guess she is deserving
Of some of my assistance

I give her clear directions
Of what to do instead
I silence her objections
My foot above my head

So don't lose motivation
As yoga can be fun
I've found my true vocation
I'll show you how it's done

*One thing led to another
and now I'm a yoga teacher*

THE FUR O'CLOCK NEWS

Today's headlines:

A MOTHER HAS GIVEN BIRTH to a record 23 kittens. The impressive litter was assembled in just under ten minutes in the hallway beside the cat bed. We caught up with the heroic Catricia Whiskerson, who said she was surprised by the experience, 'I thought my tummy was startling to feel a bit heavy. The next thing I knew, I had a family.' Catricia said that she can't wait to teach her kids how to destroy furniture. 'It's one of the first things my mum showed me – I'll definitely keep the tradition going.'

THIS JUST IN: I'm being told that a house cat has been rescued after going missing for nearly three days. The indoor Persian was discovered in a cupboard, feeling hungry and considerably well rested. Early indicators suggest that the individual was mistaken for an expensive hat. Our local correspondent approached Little Miss Placement to get her side of the storage. Speaking at her territory, the senior was quick to point the toe of blame at her humans, commenting, 'I was perfectly happy in there.'

A SPHYNX HAS TODAY LAUNCHED the world's first animal waxing salon. Animals of all kinds have been spotted queueing outside 'Bare Thrylls' to get a slice of the action. 'I didn't realise it was that colour under there,' said one satisfied customer, who wished to remain maneless. 'It was surprisingly clean inside,' oinked another on her way out. The beauty parlour isn't without its critics, with some grooming purists unwilling to accept the fly-high prices. Good Mousekeeping magazine was quick to label the concept 'a total rip-off'. Owner Shaun Rashford told our Brazilian correspondent that his new venture has been 'a dream come true,' adding, 'The first day went very smoothly.' Only time will tell if Bare Thrylls turns out to be a fairy tale, or a hairy fail.

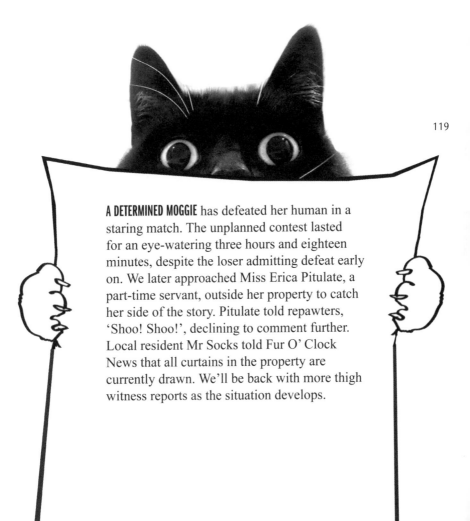

A DETERMINED MOGGIE has defeated her human in a staring match. The unplanned contest lasted for an eye-watering three hours and eighteen minutes, despite the loser admitting defeat early on. We later approached Miss Erica Pitulate, a part-time servant, outside her property to catch her side of the story. Pitulate told repawters, 'Shoo! Shoo!', declining to comment further. Local resident Mr Socks told Fur O' Clock News that all curtains in the property are currently drawn. We'll be back with more thigh witness reports as the situation develops.

FASHION AND BEAUTY

Welcome to the furry world of fashion, where the coats are glossy and the models well fed! 'You've got to hake it 'til you make it,' say the fashionistas, as fattening *is* flattering and consistently gets you ahead.

Universally admired for our natural beauty and grace, felines are the epitome of style. We've been showing humans how to be beautiful for centuries. That is, after all, why they named it the catwalk.

We make it seem easy, without relying on clothes or cosmetics to shape our look. Nude *isn't* rude – it's the look we've always pursued. But to call it *effortless* would be unfair. With our flawless reputation, the world expects to see us looking presentable on the prowl.

You don't want to be caught off guard, as you never know who might be watching. Thankfully, I've put together my top fashion and beauty tips that are certain to raise a few tails.

GET A TAN

Does your home have windows? And do you live above sea level? If you answered YES to both questions, there is a good chance that you'll have *sun puddles* in your home. Although rare in Britain, these splashes of sunlight make it all the way from the actual sun, through your windows, and on to your floor. Position yourself in one and wait to warm up. After a short while, you'll be left looking radiant. If you notice your fur starting to smoke, it's time to stop.

Show off your teeth

Is it a hiss? Is it a yawn? It's super fang! Not only does it sound impressive, but with this little hack you'll soon be attracting new admirers around the yard. When you're on the prowl, onlookers will swoon and howl as soon as they catch sight of your sharp pearly whites. Strutting around the place with a bit of tooth sticking out shows vitality and cunning – essential qualities in any stylish cat. Be careful to strike the right balance between vampire and goofy. Get that bottom lip wrong and it's over, sister.

Love your figure

Have you ever felt pressured to be a certain shape? Who could blame you, as we've long been exposed to those unrealistically lean and agile pedigrees on the cat food ads. They may look flawless from the few seconds we see them, but trust me, soon as the cameras are off, they're stuffing their faces just like us. There is nothing chic about trying to be someone else. True style is loving yourself and owning your look. So what if you can't quite fit into the bathroom sink? Take a moment each day to remind yourself that you're glorious as you are. I personally find it helpful to recite my own mantra: 'My belly is full of jelly and that is okay.'

Be shiny

There's a reason why some cats have glossier coats than others: they moisturise. It can be tricky to get hold of the right product, but you'll thank me when you do. Wait for your human to finish their shower, at which point they will begin to moisturise. Notice how they apply cream to their legs, to give you easy access. Rub against their leg to acquire as much as possible. Just to warn you, this may leave some fur stuck to your human's leg. Don't worry about this, it'll grow back. Your human will then help you massage the moisturiser into your fur using a damp cloth. You may hear a frustrated 'Ohh-wuh!!!', because they're envious of your shiny fur.

Stay clean

Do you like going outside? Perhaps you're partial to dusty surfaces? Or are you just a messy eater? Cats can get dirty in many different ways, and when we're on the catwalk, only *spotlessly* clean will suffice. Luckily, with a bit of routine upkeep you'll never fall short. The secret is simple: soon as you make contact with anything, whip out your tongue and start licking yourself. Got a sticky paw? Lick it. Food on your chest? Lick it. Muck on your back? You know the drill. Don't be afraid to plan marathon cleaning sessions in advance, as you can never overdo it. I usually schedule shower hour after meals and naps, which yields a couple of hairballs per week – and nothing screams stylish quite like clearing your throat in the corridor.

Don't stress

Do you find you're constantly rushing from one fabric surface to the next? The hectic life of a curious cat can be overwhelming, but stress is the *last* thing you need. You don't want your fur standing on end – being seen with a dishevelled coat is style suicide! It is therefore essential to take time out of your schedule to relax. Listen to your body and recognise when you've been overdoing it on the sofa. At times when you are feeling worn out, it's *okay* to say 'nah'. I know you had planned to attack the fern this evening, but it will still be there tomorrow.

Walk with your tail up

Check out that tail of yours – isn't it swish? Seriously, turn around and look at it . . . hold on . . . no, not like that . . . okay *stop spinning for a moment*! Never mind. Anyway, they call it nature's most sophisticated communication tool. I'm not sure who *they* are, but *they* are absolutely right. A lofty tail exudes curious confidence – the kind that gets you noticed. It's impossible to make the right entrance with anything else. You don't want that thing flopping around, signalling to everyone that you're a nervous wreck. Save that for the vet! Do take note, some old-fashioned cats consider a raised tail a little *exposing*. I say, 'If you've got it, flaunt it.' Stick that tail in the air like you actually care, and you shall dazzle with your derrière.

Get your beauty sleep

You're overworked. You've got a lot going on. You have commitments, places to be, staff to manage. You keep telling yourself 'I'll catch up tomorrow'. I get it. Sleep is regularly overlooked, despite being a vital part of your beauty regime. It's the nap that gets the better of you, enabling your body to properly recharge. It's your ticket to recovery after your fight with the Ginger next door. It's the honourable way to ignore your humans. Shoot for a minimum of eighteen hours a day. Any less, and you're at risk of nodding off. Take it from me: the sudden face-plant of a fatigued feline isn't a good look.

Find your accessory

Of all the ways to stand out on the prowl, nothing is quite as bold as a collar. Love them or hate them, a little bit of fabric can make a big statement. Available in a wide range of colours and materials, making a choice can be time-consuming. Do not hesitate to task your staff with finding the right design.

Reds and pinks are classic and pair brilliantly with a black coat. Blues and greys are perfect for casual, while greens and yellows can give you an edge. Choose paw-print for an ironic *I'm a pet* look, and fluorescent for safety-chic.

Why not add some sparkle with a nametag, or even a bell? It will take time to adapt the constant dinging sound wherever you go, but it's a small sacrifice for the envy of everyone in the yard. Bell-issimo!

BE YOURSELF

Being normal is never an option. If it were, you wouldn't have been born a cat. Besides, being yourself means you can do all the things *you* like doing. Perhaps you enjoy sitting on parked cars, or maybe you're more of the stay-in-and-break-stuff creature? Whatever you choose to do, make sure it's on your terms. Want to steal a sock? Take it. Don't mind your own sick? Eat it. Be yourself and never look back.

I said I could

They said I can't

I knew I would

I ate the plant

Showering will keep you young
Only if you use your tongue

Dear diary

I was stranded for days, chain-napping on a cold wooden platform, without food or water bowl. Nobody to meow at or biff in the face. Why was I there? Was I being punished? I promised myself I'll never eat another plant again, but maybe it was too late.

All I had were my thoughts, and my compulsive shower habit; it's startling just how neurotic you can become when left in solitary confinement. On a typical day I only wash myself around eighteen times, but in my plight I became obsessed. I now realise I overdid it, but it's hard to think logically with a mouth full of fur. On the plus side, my coat was sumptuously smooth.

Finally, a sliver of light. Hope. I noticed a curious parting in the wall, and an imposing figure emerging before me. Rooted to the spot with nowhere to run or hide, I was at their mercy. I watched helplessly as ten, finger-like objects bore down on me. I was slowly enveloped, sandwiched between them as they slid beneath my clammy paws. I was scooped up and out into the abyss, perhaps never to return.

It was in that wardrobe, that I discovered my true shelf.

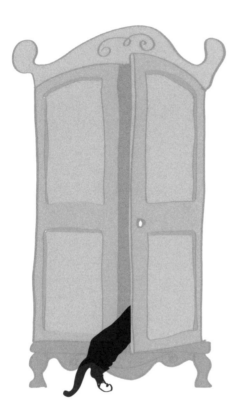

I bathe on the table
I sleep in the drawer
I play in the cupboard
I eat on the floor

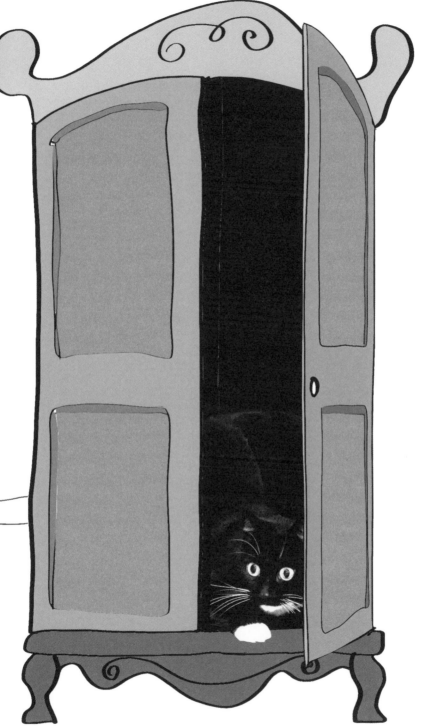

 DATING

Paws4Thought

 Hello Zelda! I see you like upholstery. I'm a big fan of textiles myself!

Great timing, I'm on the ottoman as we speak! What's your favourite fabric!?

 Let me think about that for a moment.

How about food . . . wet or dry?

 Ooh, that's a tricky one. Can I get back to you?

You know what, never mind.

ShabbyTabby

 Hi! What you up to?

I just showered. I'm about to eat a housefly.

 I have trouble catching those.

My problem is stopping at just one! Have you ever tried to hunt the red dot?

 OMC you've seen it too??

Wow, we have so much in common. Fancy a drink?

 I know a great pond. How about now?

Sure! I just need to nap, shower again, have a snack, and I'll be ready.

RESTAURANT DINING

Do you get hungry between meal times? Are you tired of eating the same food every day? If you answered YES to either question, you could be eligible for a dining experience at the best restaurant in the world. It's called 'The Neighbour's House' – it's really nearby – a bit of a modest place, but the service is second to none.

If you're lucky enough to find this secluded eatery, you may still need to earn your reservation. They don't just let in every Tom, Jack or Fluffy. Door staff tend to look favourably upon kitties in need, who are more deserving of their hospitality. You want them to take pity on you, so make sure you're collar-free when you turn up. At the entrance, try long, drawn-out meows to indicate hunger. If you're well-groomed and curvy, they may not buy it, in which case try rolling in a puddle before they see you. They don't need to know how it happened.

Once you're inside The Neighbour's House, you'll notice that there aren't any menus laying around. Everything is made to order, so just tell the chef what you're after. Play your claws right, and it won't be long before you're gobbling up a bowl of tuna. Unless of course you've stumbled upon their trendy new vegan branch. The choices there are relatively limited, but don't leave without trying the baby chicken peas.

Garden hopping

Did you know that humans aren't allowed in each other's gardens? And, if one human should be found in another human's garden without prior invitation, they could be asked to leave!? Some haven't been in another human's garden in years. Others have barely even climbed a fence. Such is the madness of the many suburban humans who refrain from garden-hopping.

One of the best things about being a cat is that we have access to everyone's gardens. We don't need to ask if we can sit on your patch of grass. Whether we fancy hunting in your pond or using your lawn as a toilet, we decide how the adventure unfolds.

Climbing a fence takes a bit of practice. They vary in height and grip, and some are harder to access than others. If you're not feeling confident, try running up the wardrobe first. In any case, it is essential that you switch off gravity before any attempt is made. Soon as you reach the top, you can take a chance and leap into the next garden. If, however, you are feeling indecisive, just sit on the fence.

Get stuck in a tree

Are you feeling ignored? Do you need an ego boost? Well, look no further than that big tree outside! Many cats don't get the attention they deserve, and if you're one of them, the solution to your problem is only a climb away. All you need is a set of claws and some confidence. Soon as you finish your nap, bolt outside and head for your chosen tree. Sink your claws into the bark and scramble in an upwards direction.

Once you hit the first set of branches, be very careful not to think of the consequences. Tree-climbing can be daunting, so it's important to stay positive and remind yourself, *the only way is up!* Push yourself to new heights, leaping to each impending branch until you can go no further. When you reach the top, steady yourself on your perch and survey your territory. Look out for the first unwitting human who notices you from the ground below – if you've followed my instructions, they should look *really* small!

You are now playing a waiting game, as a curious cat design flaw prevents you from making your own way down. Observe the crowd of humans forming to show their admiration for your ascent. Listen for the crescendo of sirens as your rescue team approach. Finally, greet the member of staff who emerges to escort you out of the tree to a heroes' welcome. The entire neighbourhood applauds your courage and you become the talk of the town. Not bad for a Thursday afternoon.

I do a climb
I'm in a tree
I wait some time
They rescue me

137

Dear diary

Having spent a lot of time with footwear, shoelaces have become a big part of my life. But despite collecting and nibbling on them for years, I've never quite known where they come from. I vaguely recall my mother telling me that shoelaces were found in shops, but I've always dismissed the fantasy. Until now.

Earlier, I noticed that my humans had left the living room window open. Although it wasn't my normal exit point, I thought I should at least investigate. Upon landing on the turf outside, I was unfamiliar with my surroundings. I began to explore, skittering further away from base and deep into uncharted territory, crossing creeks and weaving through woodland. Until I found an opening.

I crept out and a long cobbled street stretched before me into the distance. There were neither trees nor houses, except a tiny building at the very end. I thought I should turn around and head back, but curiosity got the better of me and I soon found myself at the front door.

'Herrrrow?' I inquired.

No answer.

'HERRRRRRROWW!?' I asked again.

Then I noticed the cat flap, and so I went inside.

There were shoelaces everywhere! Stacked up high on the shelves and hanging low from the ceiling. Blacks and browns and yellows and pinks, waxed or braided in all lengths and thicknesses.

'Need any shoelaces?' called an eager voice.

I slinked my way to the back of the shop, each shoelace gently stroking my face, swinging back and forth in my wake. Not a shoe in sight.

One shoelace stood out to me: it was light brown, round and a medium thickness. 'What a beauty!' I thought, as I batted it around with my paw.

'That's on special at the moment – buy one get one free,' said the shopkeeper, poking his head through a cluster of shoelaces.

I stood up on my hind legs and gave it a sniff. I was gobsmacked. 'This is the one.'

'Let me get you a box,' he whispered.

The shopkeeper climbed up his ladder and disappeared into a dimly lit room, where he was audibly moving many things around, muttering to himself every few minutes.

Eventually he reappeared, dragging behind him a particularly long, thin and very smart looking box. He paused for a moment and shot me a wide and toothy grin. He then carried on to the till.

'That'll be £1.99.'

My heart sank. Having found the perfect shoelace, I couldn't give him anything in return. I thought long and hard as the shopkeeper slowly drummed his fingers on the counter. Finally, an idea struck.

'Stick it on the tab?' I yelped.

'Very well!'

The human handed me the box, which we carefully threaded through the store and out the cat flap, and I headed back. I was so elated, skipping and skating along, that I barely remembered the route home.

The next thing I knew, I was back in the living room, curled up in a ball on the floor. I looked over my haunches and noticed that the window was firmly shut. This was puzzling. I got up to investigate, but something tripped me up. As I looked down, I saw a shoelace! It was light brown, round and a medium thickness. 'What a beauty!' I thought, as I batted it around with my paw.

Dear Zelda,

Why does my cat ignore me? I'm always attentive to him, making sure he is fed in a timely manner with frequent treats in between. I give him all the cat toys he could ever need, and I'm ready whenever he wants to be petted or brushed.

Despite this, he barely even acknowledges me when I come home. I'll call his name in the sweetest voice: 'Mister Pebbles?' and yet he doesn't even turn his head to look at me. Is he purposely avoiding me? Is it because of the time I told him off for bringing a mouse inside?

I obviously love him to bits, so please help me Zelda. My dressing gown is barely getting any action.

Yours faithfully,

Iggy Nord

I had intended to answer this letter, but my search for a pen led me to the sofa. It was at this point that I thought, scratch that.

I heard my human call my name
I didn't want to go
I wonder why he needed me
I guess I'll never know

CAREERS ZELDA THE POPSTAR

I'm always listening to the radio in the kitchen – not by choice, mind you. Over time, I have noticed that cats are not fairly represented in songs. Usually the lyrics are about humans and their interests, which doesn't seem relevant. While I was napping on a blanket one afternoon, the idea struck me: 'What about a covers band?'

I started making some notes, and before I knew it, I'd written my own album! I haven't recorded it yet as I'm still waiting for a record label and soundproofing in the bathroom. For now, here are some of my defining lyrics:

'Wise men say
Only fools rush in
But I can't help
Napping in living room'
Elvis Purrsley

'If you liked it then you should have put a string on it'
Meowncé

"Cus maybe
You're gonna be the one that saves me
'Cus after all
You're my favourite wall'
Oahiss

'I got 99 problemth and my tongue ith one'
Lay-Z

'You're a little late
Couch already torn'
Catalie Imbruglia

'It's late in the evening
She's wondrin' what clothes to tear
She puts on her meowkup
And washes her rectum hair'
Eric Lapton

'I like big bugs and I cannot lie'
Sir meow-a-lot

'When I get that feeling, it's like, bugs on the ceiling'
Marvin Stray

'Is this the real life? Is this just fantasy?
Caught on the worktop, no escape from apology . . . '
Freddie Meowcury

'Eat. Sleep. Panic. Repeat.'
Catboy Slim, Riva Purr & Feedyman

'If you wanna be my tuna, you gotta get in my bowl'
Mice Girls

'My tailshake brings all the toms to the yard'
Kelhiss

'There's no business like throw business'
Irving Purrlin

'All you knead is loaf'
The Beatles

Dear diary

I had my first date last night! ShabbyTabby was at my front door by dusk as we agreed. I watched him from the window, just to check that he was who he said he is. He was definitely a bit shorter than he had put on his profile. As he reached the door, he walked head first into the cat flap. I forgot to mention that it's microchip.

Visibly embarrassed, he started mewing for me and pawing at the door. I rushed downstairs and out the flap to greet him. He turned around to let me sniff him first, which I appreciated. He did have a bit of a weird tail, but he'd clearly made an effort. He soon scurried off ahead of me. I found it quite hard to keep pace, as there were more fences than he'd let on.

The pond he took me to was . . . well, more of a marsh. No fish to speak of, though the rushes did look pretty blowing in the evening breeze. We had a drink but he didn't offer to catch dinner.

He walked me home afterwards. I thought of inviting him in for a spider. When we reached the porch, he stopped and blinked at me slowly. I panicked and flew through the cat flap. I think I handled that really well.

CLOSE TO MY HEART

All still. No speech.
I jump. No reach.
At night. I scare.
Look up. Yur there.
                    – Ceiling

148

Thin hands. White face.
Round head. One place.
You tock. You tick.
I watch. I lick.

                    – Alarm Clock

Such width. Such height.
Much still. Much bright.
So flat. So clear.
No chat. No fear.
                    – Window

New Carpet

Here's a story of my plight
Which left me feeling bitter
A messy morning full of fright
Against a carpet fitter

Just before the work commenced
I found a place to hang
Suddenly my body tensed
I heard the loudest bang

I scurried to another room
The closest I could find
I worried that I'd met my doom
My food bowl left behind.

As the fitter ripped and knocked
Of one thing I was certain
The evil critter hadn't clocked
Me spying from the curtain

Out of sight for hours on end
I hadn't slept all day
The carpet man was not our friend
He turned our carpet grey!

Finally the beast had fled
I knew that I would win
'Soon' I muttered to myself
The scratching will begin!

I cannot lie
I must confide
I do a bad
And then I hide

Dear diary

Prison. Everyone imagines it, but no one believes they'll have to go. Nobody thinks they would ever do anything bad enough to get locked up. But things can happen when you least expect them, and your life can change in an instant. Was it because I broke into the airing cupboard? Or maybe that time I raided the compost bin? It was hard to understand while being forced into my chamber by the merciless guards on duty. When you take those first steps in your cell room and the door clips shut, it's really happening.

I knew that prison cells were uncomfortable, but nobody prepared me for this. The loneliness. The darkness. The tight squeeze; it was the underwear drawer all over again. Not to mention the smells! It absolutely reeked of wee – luckily my own. There were no food bowls, nor furnishings to scratch. Just my blanket; my familiar fabric, home to all those pheromones I'd harvested over the years. When you've lost everything, you value the simple things. My blanket was here for me, like he always has been.

Prison can play tricks with your mind. When you're locked away, you can't help but reflect on your life and all of your missed opportunities. 'If only I had eaten more tuna.' 'If only I had devoured more salmon.' 'If only I had inhaled more cod.' I could barely finish listing all of my unrequited fish desires before I was abruptly thrown against the wall. My cell rose up off the ground and we were on the move.

I noticed that I was moving, and yet my legs were not. I panicked, scratching in every direction while informing the entire planet that I was in danger.

Then, I saw the man in the white coat. He had a smile, but he was not my friend. Was I being assessed? Did they have concerns for my sanity? I knew I shouldn't have been caught licking the windows at home. It was too late. The crazy bus had arrived and I had a one-way ticket.

The man in the white coat hoisted me onto a cold metal surface. His gloves felt clammy against my fur. I could tell he was almost as nervous as me. His petting skills left a lot to be desired, as he prodded and poked me in a number of restricted areas. It wasn't long before he fished out a threateningly thin implement and approached me from behind. In one swift movement, I felt the icy spike inside me, followed by a short beep.

'Okay Zelda?'

I was not okay. I was a furry Popsicle and nobody wanted to lick me.

Just then, I detected a familiar scent. The door swung open – it was my humans! They were here to negotiate my release! I had hoped they would come to my rescue after all I've done for them. After a lengthy discussion with the man in the white coat, they had reached an agreement. The humans handed over what must have been a large ransom. Perhaps I shouldn't have questioned their loyalty, even if it was a relatively minor fee to have me discharged. I like to think most humans would do the same for their boss?

Miss the jump
See the vets
Back at home
No regrets

154

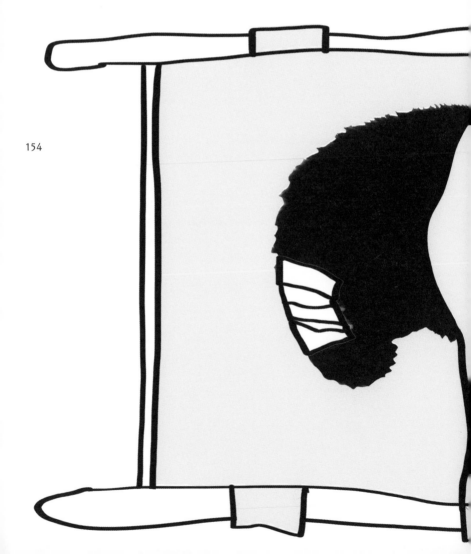

DATING

ShorthairedBrit

 Hlelo

 *Hello! (sorry, tail got in the way)

Haha, I can relate

 Wow, your eyes are so big!

156

Oh I just have a tiny head

 Ah. So what are you looking for?

I don't know. I've never really done this before.

 Me too. Maybe we could find out together?

Dear diary

I met a handsome cat tonight. He was British and had short hair, but I couldn't remember the breed. He was a lot cleaner than ShabbyTabby and had a nice meow.

I had suggested going somewhere casual for a couple of water bowls, but he insisted on The Wheely Bin. He clearly wanted to impress me. Queues were horrendous but we managed to get a spot right by the lid. As we tucked into our left'oeuvres he told me a bit about his recent flea treatment. The conversation was otherwise sparse, which was a shame because he did have really nice jowls.

As we left the restaurant, he purred and looked me directly in the eyes. He was so well-groomed. As I leaned in for a sniff, a hairball flew out of my mouth! I was so embarrassed. He brushed it off, but I just wanted to run home and hide under the stairs.

In the end I made an excuse and sprinted up a nearby tree. Took me ages to find my way down, but luckily the grass broke my fall.

CAREERS

ZELDA THE PAWLITICIAN

I am proud to say that I'm going to become a pawlitician.

I already have extensive experience in the cabinet.

158

VOTE ZELDA!

- Legalise mouse hunting
- Revolutionise transport links to Cape Cod
- Increase distribution of fur clumps at ground level
- Legalise snoozing at work
- Enable all cats to invest in the sock market
- Fill every nursing home with a hundred cats
- Launch a free re-stuffing scheme for all soft furnishings
- Deliver a cat-bed disposal scheme
- Replace VAT with CAT
- Build a revolutionary cardboard eco village
- Enforce a minimum-carpeted area in all homes
- Install cat flaps in all public buildings
- Remove doors to all public buildings
- Upgrade all cat TVs to double glazing
- Ban thermometers in all veterinary clinics

ONE WEEK TO GO

With my manifesto drafted, all I had to do was launch my campaign. At a lavish invite-only event by the water bowl, I set out my bold vision for the future. My speech was enthusiastically received, and I had to pause several times for rapturous gurgling from the sink.

I've heard that all successful modern campaigns are built on strong fundraising. I set to work immediately, listing a large number of unnecessary items I found throughout our home on fleaBay. I'm pleased to report that I've already had several bids for our TV.

I dedicated the rest of the day to strategy. At first there was some reluctance to tackle the elephant in the room, but eventually the issue of voter fraud came up. Squirrels are the obvious concern; those secretive tree-dwellers are only out for themselves.

By the time I emerged from a closed-door meeting in the fridge I was cold and hungry. Pawlitics takes extraordinary stamina – I've already had to abandon several of my mid-morning naps just to get anything done. I'm so behind on my normal duties that the house barely looks lived in.

The Campaign Trail

While many of my best pawlicies are aspirational, I'm anxious that I might be out of touch. I had to get out there and talk to real voters.

The first stop of the day was a focus group on kitchen table issues. I soon found out that ours is a bit wobbly. I was disappointed that both participants were human as they can't vote, but I decided to go ahead anyway. Discussion mostly revolved around bread and butter policies, the current milk shortage, and squabbling about who would take out the recycling. They seemed to lack the imagination to engage with my platform, despite some impassioned mewing on my part.

After a quick nap, I left my office to meet with some grassroots supporters. I returned from the garden having dug up precious little, so I cleared my schedule and went back out on the road. This was also of limited value, and I collapsed dejectedly on top of the shoe rack.

Later that day it hit me – the answer was right under my nose! It turns out that shoes are quite opinionated, though they're concerned mostly with weatherproofing and other routine maintenance. Nonetheless, it was a useful canvassing session. There was a lot of support for my position on fish stocks – we can all agree on the pressing need for fresh soles. Sadly they couldn't be suede to take any concrete steps. I decided that shoes fundamentally lack perspective, and despite my commitment to help the downtrodden I was better off focusing on my core voters.

The Greater Good

Some rival campaign literature arrived this morning. I found it by the front door. It's unclear who's behind it, but I had to admit it was ruthlessly calculated. Page after page tugged on the heartstrings with glossy pictures of perfect couches, side chairs and other soft furnishings, looking to buy votes with offers of free financing.

With the threat of late competition brewing, I hastily assembled my campaign team for an emergency strategy meeting on top of the dresser. However unrealistic, it's unlikely that my rival's false promises would be exposed until after the election. If I was to see off this new opponent, I had to broaden my appeal.

So I spent the afternoon knocking on doors (notorious swing voters). My political career now hinged on their support. Thankfully, the exit poll showed signs of a late rebound. It had been a busy day, and I had to dash to make an evening campaign rally several rooms away. Standing beside the television, I gave an emotional speech to the assembled crowd. They watched intently, only leaving the room to get up for a snack as my address reached its inspiring climax.

Election Day

I set out early on Election Day. I'd barely managed fourteen hours of sleep and was a total wreck. I descended into the voting ottoman with a heavy heart: had I done enough? I emerged from the darkness several hours later, refreshed but resigned to my fate. It was all in the voters' paws now.

The polls closed at dinnertime, and I awaited the results with baited breath. I counted and recounted the ballot paper several times. The tally was the same every time – I had won! By one whole vote! I could barely contain my excitement. Now that I was an elected pawlitician, I had a real opportunity to make a difference. I started by rewarding my loyal campaign staff with a deep purr followed up by a headbutt. They seemed to like that.

I immediately wrote to Pawliament to inform them of my impressive victory, and received a note of congratulations from the chair. I'm waiting on confirmation of exactly which bench I'll be sitting on. Claws crossed it's the one in the living room by the fireplace.

Dear Zelda,

My cat insists on bringing dead animals into the house. No matter how much I try to dissuade him, I regularly come home to find some kind of crime scene on the floor.

In the past, Fluffles would occasionally bring in a mouse, but lately the problem seems to be getting worse. Last week he captured a squirrel, and just yesterday, a live magpie! I'm terrified of what he'll find next – *could* a fox fit through our cat flap!?

Sometimes his kills are barely distinguishable as I'm reduced to mopping up assorted entrails from the carpet. I suspect he's eating them as he's barely interested in the food I'm serving him.

Please help me Zelda. Our local wildlife depends on it.

Yours powerlessly,

Ms Dressing McGowan

Dear Ms McGowan,

I was surprised to receive a letter of this nature, as it seems you are interpreting these gifts negatively. I can only presume that you are either confused or very ungrateful. I'm also quite confused as to how you humans are managing to contact me.

For your convenience, I have laid out the following system to explain the meaning behind Fluffles' offerings:

Whole animal = highest honour

Half an animal = I got distracted

Remnants = I'm upset but I still love you

I hope this helps clarify matters. If you are still oblivious, kindly reply to this message with a sample attached.

Best fishes,

Zelda

I lay awake as my human cried
'Why did you bring this bird inside!?'

INFAMOUS
CAT CRIMINALS

2' 0"
1' 6"
1' 0"
0' 6"

Blackwhiskers the Pirate

Originally a ship's cat, Blackwhiskers was drawn to the New World by the promise of adventure and all the rats he could eat. After months at sea, he grew tired of his duties and mutinied, taking a ship for his own. Under its new command, the Golden Tom raided Spanish vessels, ruthlessly plundering them for their salted fish and other tapas. Feared throughout the Caribbean, Blackwhiskers was only held back by his intense dislike for water. He was finally captured and declawed after a drawn out battle, interrupted only by frequent naps from both sides.

Jack the Slipper

In 1888, London lived in fear of this legendary cereal spiller. Known for his clumsiness, he would accidentally claw at birds or trip over squirrels as he tumbled his way through the trees under cover of darkness. He famously startled a dog to death in an alleyway when he unexpectedly slammed into a dustbin. Jack was so embarrassed about his criminal lack of poise and grace that he went to extraordinary lengths to conceal his identity, which to this day remains a mystery.

WANTED

'BILLY THE KITTEN'

★ REWARD ★

3 SALMON

Age, 18 months. Height, 8 inches.
American Shorthair.

Leader of the worst band of fangsters the
Territory has ever had to deal with. The above
reward will be paid for his capture.

★★★ FED AND ALIVE ★★★

BILLY THE KITTEN

One of the most feared cats in the Wild West, Billy the kitten was responsible for a string of offences in the late nineteenth century. Originally employed as a meowboy in Lincoln, New Mexico, Billy would work long hours rounding up mice for a pittance. Struggling to make ends meet, he turned to a life of violence and robbery. Billy made a name for himself when he held up a fish wagon at just fifteen months old, landing him in the county jailhouse. He escaped two days later and fled town with a gang of outclaws, getting into scrapes and standoffs in numerous territories they passed through. Billy became the most wanted cat in the West, as Sheriff Pat Furrett tracked him for months in pursuit of his capture. Furrett eventually found Billy hiding in a saloon under a piano stool, resulting in one of history's most intense hissy fits.

Pablo Escopurr

Pablo Escopurr was a Colombian rug lord who clawed his way to prominence in the 1970s. Escopurr founded the infamous Bedlinen Cartel – a highly disorganised Colombian rug ring. He became a key influence in the international trafficking of jute, whose versatile uses for scratching posts, string and rug making were the fabric of his wealth. Escopurr had a brief stint in pawlitics, gaining nationwide support from street cats in his provision of catnip for local communities. Rugs, however, took priority, and his monopoly of the market threatened to put Carpet Right out of business.

The government challenged the legality of Escopurr's dealings after discovering a number of his assets stashed behind the sofa. The clawthorities negotiated with him to stop all criminal activity in exchange for a reduced prison sentence and preferential treatment. As a result, Escopurr built 'La Catedral' – his own luxury pet carrier, guarded by Bedlinen staff in a remote corridor surrounded by cat trees. He escaped after a brief stay, spending the rest of his life hiding in bushes, scratching anyone who encroached.

Escopurr's name was cemented in mainstream popular culture in 2015, following the launch of his TV show on Petflix. The series exposed his many crimes as well as a more cuddly side to his character. Escopurr is regarded by some felines today as a modern-day Robin Hood, although many remain on the fence. How could a cat so sweet be so ruthless?

AL CAPAWN

Al Capawn was one of the most notorious fangsters in American history, who rose to infamy terrorizing Brooklyn wildlife during the 1920s prohibitten era. Often confused with Spanish fish-gobbler El Caprawn, Al Capawn was nicknamed 'Clawface' following a showdown with a Maine Coon who lived across the road. He built a reputation as a merciless mouser and hissy fit starter, getting into over a thousand fights with cats around the neighbourhood. His disputes with rival fangsters were mostly territorial, as he was hell-bent on claiming the next-door neighbour's garden. His humans eventually moved to a more secluded property where Capawn led a slower pace of life. There, he became a devoted lap cat, and was pampered with all the treats and chin rubs he ever wanted.

Missed Chances

Here's a story of regret
About a meal I didn't get
A night of feeling unfulfilled
With many friendships to rebuild

It was a chilly London day
The humans out til late
For many hours they'd been away
Indifferent to my fate

To myself I'd mostly kept
The time I hadn't clocked
'Meow,' I cried 'I've overslept'
And then the door unlocked

HUMANS? Were they getting near?
I'd smelled them from afar
DINNER? Was it really here?
The door was soon ajar

Racing down the stairs I went
To greet them as I do
Prompted by their awful scent
Back up the stairs I flew

Through the banister I pounced
While clawing at their hair
'Stop it Zelda!' they announced
(I nearly made them swear)

I heard my belly rumbling loud
A pain I couldn't bear
'Why is Zelda grumbling now?'
My humans didn't care

I noticed that they had a bag
And suddenly I thought
'Perhaps it's food that I can snag'
And this is why we fought

They put it on the counter top
To keep it out of sight
But I'm a cat you cannot stop
I braced myself for flight

Towards the bag I did a leap
I swiped it with my paw
I slipped and landed in a heap
The bag fell on the floor

The food exploded on the deck
It happened in a flash
My humans sprinted in to check
I thought I'd better dash

I hoped I would remain unseen
If I could be discreet
Yet right before I fled the scene
I stole a piece of meat

Just as I was heading out
I heard my humans flip
The meat was safely in my mouth
But then I lost my grip

I sensed my humans were upset
I chose to hide away
Although this meal I didn't get
I'll try another day

DATING

SportyBengal

Roses are red
Hairballs are grey
I made one for you
It's in the hallway

Please don't contact me ever again.

Catfish4U

Good day. Am an honest, genuine cat looking for a serious relationship. I was just closing my account when suddenly I saw your profile and I instantly fell in love.

Hai! You sound amazing and totally trustworthy. Loved your photos – your litter tray looks enormous!

Am looking for my soulmate, so please kindly contact me on my personal email as I will like to know you better: realcatlove@hot-tail.com.

Something smells fishy.

Also I'm not sure about this.
Let me nap on it, k?

FerociousFred

 Hai. Nice photos – that squirrel looks terrified!

 Hey thanks, I guess I got lucky.

 I liked your photos too. How come there's a shrimp on your head?

 Oh that's Crusty! He's a friend.

 Ahhh okay. So what's your poetry about?

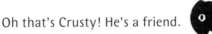 There's lots about furniture, plants, and life in general.

 I LOVE furniture! Plants are tasty too.

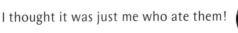 I thought it was just me who ate them!

 Same! How about we take this conversation outside?

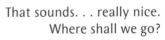 That sounds. . . really nice. Where shall we go?

Why don't we see where our noses take us?

ZELDA THE ASTRONAUT

I looked up at the sky one night
Surprised by what I saw
So many shiny dots in sight
Of this I was in awe

My sighting left me mesmerised
I'd found a special place!
And gradually I realised
It looked a bit like space

I've always dreamt of visiting
I've longed to make the trip
I know I'll find it interesting
I only need a ship

I'll search the house extensively
To find the right machine
It needs to work effectively
And must not cause a scene

The humans cannot see me leave
They wouldn't understand
They often say that I'm naïve
I'll call them when I land

I'm new to being an astronaut
But please don't be alarmed
I've given this a lot of thought
I will return unharmed

The time has come for me to go
Can't wait another day
I'll tell the moon you said hello
And steal the Milky Way

MEOWCURY

PURRTO

MEWPITUR

Following the success of my pawlitical campaign, I've yearned to have a greater influence on the world. I feel it is time I set my sights on a higher purpose, where I am no longer limited to earthbound adventures. Despite my local achievements, I cannot rest on my laurels. I'll therefore be reducing my sleep to sixteen hours per day to pursue a career as an astronaut. Such a radical change to my routine is necessary, for there are many other cat planets waiting to discover the virtues of a life lived curiously.

A job of this scale can't be done alone, so I'm inviting you to join me on my voyage. Together, we furry adventurers will inspire the mewniverse! *'What about my humans?'* I hear you ask. By now they should be qualified to fulfil their basic duties with a little less supervision, although there are a few things to consider in advance of your trip:

EARTH

While you're hurtling through the catmosphere, your humans may wonder where you are. It could be useful to consult them before you set off. Spaceships are complex machines with many different settings, so it is important that the humans receive some basic training. After all, every expedition needs competent ground crew at mission control.

VENHISS

Just got a job with NASA

They hired me to stare into space

NEPTUNA

SATURN-THE-MAT

Sit down together on the kitchen floor and discuss which spin cycle is optimal, as well as any garments to leave in the cylinder. I would generally recommend setting your vessel to 'Delicates' for long journeys, and 'Eco mode' if it's just a quick trip to the moon. Whichever you choose, make sure that the door to your capsule remains firmly closed between planets.

MEOWS

Your humans may have some reservations about you leaving, as they risk losing their sense of purpose in your absence. If you sense any hesitation, offer reassurance by rubbing yourself against them until they are covered in fur. You can always keep them busy by creating a mess around the home.

181

Depending on your direction of travel, space can get quite cold. Be sure to pack throws and blankets if they are not already in the cylinder. This can also improve comfort during transit.

Before launch, it is sensible to free up your calendar by rescheduling any upcoming meetings or naps. Based on my experience, I would also recommend using the litter tray prior to departure.

Upon arrival, take a moment to get used to the changes in gravity, as you may find it trickier to land on your feet. When exploring planets on foot you'll need to be tethered to your ship, so check that you have packed plenty of string. Keep an eye out for the floating space tuna, and if you do feel overwhelmed at any time, just press paws.

FURANUS

One small step for man . . .
One giant blep for catkind.

Dear diary

It was a long walk to my spaceship. I padded nervously across the kitchen tiles, agonising about everything I was about to leave behind, most of which was under the sofa. As I stood in front of my capsule, I realised my life may never be the same again, but I had made my decision. I slowly lifted my paw, and I licked it.

I repeated the process a number of times, as I wanted to look my best in case Fur O'Clock were covering the launch. It had been a while since the last cat went to space, and I knew my enterprise may raise a few hairballs. The great Fuzz Aldrin once said, 'Meows is there, waiting to be reached.' With this in mind, I hopped into the washing machine and hoped for the best.

During final system checks, we hit a snag. One of the ground crew raced over waving to me to call off the flight, as there appeared to be an issue with the oxygen supply. As I climbed out of my ship, I realised that I may have been a little hasty, and there were further calculations to make before lift-off. I also noticed that we were in danger of encroaching on dinnertime. I had to make a tough decision, and after much deliberation, I opted to postpone the trip.

It had been a long and emotional day, and although I didn't manage to get to space, my meal was an absolute blast.

Top 10

RATIONAL FEARS FOR CATS

One advantage of being a startled cat is that every fear is totally justified. I know I'm barely scratching the surface, but here's my top 10 rational fears:

1. Aluminium foil

Cling Film's evil twin, used to construct a barrier between cats and leftovers. Aluminium foil is abnormally loud for something so thin. All it takes is one tiny kink in this mystic material and you have a thunderstorm. Avoid unless already rolled into a ball.

2. The mirror

Noticing your reflection for the first time can be a scary experience. Not only is it staggering to discover that you are a cat, but your subsequent expressions can be startling. If you're not careful, you're almost certain to trigger an existential crisis! Who would blame you, as the aptly named 'Catoptrophobia' is a recognised and entirely rational fear. Unavoidable.

3. The doorbell

Doorbells signal the arrival of unfamiliar humans – because no animal aside from a human is capable of operating a doorbell. Except maybe a horse. But have you ever seen a horse at your front door? Why not? Anyway, just be warned that doorbell anxiety is real. Should a doorbell sound at a time when you are not expecting it (which is every time), find a dark, sheltered crevice, and squeeze yourself into it for at least one calendar month.

4. The Hairdryer

A confused vacuum cleaner with the ability to create an indoor hurricane. Typically used as a form of personal torture, this unpredictable device can make your human hot-headed. Easily avoided by recruiting staff who are bald or live in a tent.

5. Being petted badly

Some humans pet cats too softly, too firmly, too slowly, too quickly, or at the wrong time, or in the wrong place. Many won't let you sniff their hand first, and some are daring enough to make contact below the neck. Avoid by fleeing or clinging to their face.

6. Silence

As any startled cat will tell you, silence is the hallmark of awkwardness. Experience silence for too long and silence will simply get louder. Escape by howling or sleeping at all times.

7. Cucumbers

Famous for sneaking up on you when you're eating, these snakes of the vegetable world only move when your back is turned. Though yet to actually attack a cat, the odds of a cucumber ambush are increasing with every passing day. Avoid by emigrating to the bookshelf.

8. Water

One of the greatest hazards known to cats. According to science, if your fur is exposed to water, it could make you wet. This presents a huge threat to your beauty regime and overall comfort. Unless you are drinking or spilling it, you must avoid water at all costs. Stick to covering yourself in your own saliva instead, which is the safest way to stay soggy.

9. Balloons

Claws and thin rubber don't get along. I found out the hard way, as a seemingly harmless game of *biff the thing* led to a nuclear explosion. Don't make the same mistake, fur pals. Avoid all humans currently celebrating a birthday, or able to tie a knot.

10. Balloon animal artists

See above. Those who choose to ignore the dangers of balloons cannot be trusted. Should you be unlucky enough to face such a human, turn around immediately and stick your tail in the air. By showing off your very own balloon knot, you'll surely take their breath away.

AGONY AUNT

Dear Zelda,

Although my staff are generally attentive to my needs, they are sometimes absent from home for long periods of time without explanation. I hadn't realised the extent of the problem before, but last week this happened five days in a row. Surely grounds for dismissal!

Admittedly this mostly occurs during napping hours, but still — what if I were to wake up and want a snack?

Paws truly,

Perkins

Dear Perkins,

In my experience, you get out what you put in. Your staff must be reminded of their obligations. They are there to provide for your needs first and theirs second.

The most productive way forward is to make it harder for them to leave the house. In some cases, remaining on their lap will be sufficient. However, if they are determined to disregard your orders, you'll need to take more direct action. Stand between them and the door, and stare at them disapprovingly. If that doesn't do the trick, hide their equipment. Shoes are a great place to start — it seems humans are very reluctant to go outside without them.

If you hear phrases like 'where are my keys?' or the magic words 'missed my train', you'll know you're making progress.

Best fishes,

Zelda

Dear diary

I woke up in a panic. This time it was because I had overslept, and Fred was going to be here soon! I had barely twenty minutes to shower, so I just gave my paws a quick once-over and hoped for the best.

Fred waited for me under the lamp post by the gate. He wore a loose-fitting grey collar with a silver bell. He was a big tom, who lumbered along beside me as we walked to dinner. 'We're here,' he meowed. He'd picked the perfect paving slab.

He asked me what I'd like for dinner. I was in the mood for mouse. He was only off for a few minutes before returning with almost a whole one! We ended up sharing the kill, batting it back and forth. I'd never eaten with someone before, which took some guts. Then I noticed he had a bit of tail caught in his whiskers. I reached in and brushed it away for him. He felt warm.

The conversation flowed almost naturally and we decided to move on to a nearby brick wall. The cars were out, and we sat together watching them go by. Then it hit me – it had been ages since my last freakout. Somehow with Fred I was a little less skittish.

The Night was fast coming to a close and I had to get back to wake my humans. Fred saw me to the front gate, where we stopped for a moment. Just when I was about to climb over, he licked me on the cheek. I stared back at him intensely as he turned and prowled away down the street. I felt a quiver in my tail. Could Fred be the kind of cat I'd rub my face on one day? I have no idea where this adventure might lead, but I do know one thing – I'm curious.

Staying Curious

I want to share with you a rhyme
I've given it some thought
Holy shrimp! Is that the time?
I guess I'll keep this short

When my humans rescued me
I was extremely skittish
I didn't like confronting things
(Perhaps because I'm British)

I had to face some challenges
While anxious and fatigued
But humans persevered with me
And I became intrigued

I'd watch them from a secret spot
It's true that I was frightened
But when I was observing them
My every sense was heightened!

I realised life can be intense
And though it may be stirring
Embrace it all without defence
And soon you will be purring

I know it's easier shred than done
I'm not the greatest coach
But many problems can be fun
By changing your approach

Certain things will startle you
And some things will be boring
Don't fixate on *what* you do
It's *how* you go exploring

If you believe a plan is flawed
It may not be complete
Go right back to the clawing board
And don't admit defeat!

For all the times you do a bad
Your humans may be furious
But thankfully you can be glad
As you were being curious

So never be too careful
And never know too much
And if you like adventures
I hope we stay in touch

Acknowledgements

I've spent many hours staring back at Zelda, trying to figure out what she's saying. I've shared this process with someone truly special, who plays a big role in translating Zelda's mewsings: thank you Caroline, my brilliant wife (and Zelda's yoga student), for your ideas and encouragement. You've been so accommodating when I needed space, and insightful when Zelda travelled to space.

Huge thanks to my brother Simon, for your furmidable contribution to the writing and creative direction. I'm so lucky to be related to you. Thank you Mum & Dad for creating Simon (seriously, bravo) and for giving me the confidence to pursue my dreams.

A thousand meows for my agent Juliet Mushens, who helped me find the purrfect publisher. From the first conversation with my editor, Rhiannon Smith, I knew we'd create something unique, and I couldn't imagine a more enthusiastic and witty human to make it happen. Please save a shoelace for our superb cover designer, Nico Taylor, and extend belly rubs to Hannah, Louise, Aimee, India and the rest of the wonderful staff at Little, Brown.

One tin of sustainable line-caught tuna for Jenny Parrot, who believed in me, and introduced me to Juliet. A gold tin opener for the Mayhew rescue shelter – I cannot thank you enough for introducing me to Zelda.

I owe astonishing amounts of fish to Emil and Sian at D.R.ink, who designed and illustrated the most beautiful book. You went beyond expectations, and I'm proud of the Zelda-world you've created.

An endless ball of string for everyone following @CuriousZelda on Twitter, Facebook and Instagram. Thank you for liking and sharing Zelda, and for all your comments, poetry and fan-art. I hope you love this book. You bring me so much joy, and I have saved space for all of you in the sock drawer.

Lastly, thank you Zelda. You're an inspiration, and you're the friend I've always wanted. Thank you for keeping my forearms warm while I type, and long may your adventures continue.